Managing Intellectual Property

Chris Fitzsimmons and Tim Jones

- ■ Fast track route to managing and exploiting intellectual property

- ■ Covers the key areas of managing IPR from the alternative forms available and their means of protection to approaches for creating revenue and leveraging value

- ■ Examples and lessons from some of the world's most successful businesses, including BTG, IBM, Qualcomm and the Teletubbies, and ideas from the smartest thinkers, including Kevin Rivette, Jessica Litman, Thomas Stewart and Seth Shulman

- ■ Includes a glossary of key concepts and a comprehensive resources guide

essential management thinking at your fingertips

Copyright © Capstone Publishing 2002

The right of Chris Fitzsimmons and Tim Jones to be identified as the authors of this work has been asserted in accordance with the Copyright, Designs and Patents Act 1988

First published 2002 by
Capstone Publishing (a Wiley company)
8 Newtec Place
Magdalen Road
Oxford OX4 1RE
United Kingdom
http://www.capstoneideas.com

All rights reserved. Except for the quotation of short passages for the purposes of criticism and review, no part of this publication may be reproduced, stored in a retrieval system, or transmitted, in any form or by any means, electronic, mechanical, photocopying, recording or otherwise, without the prior permission of the publisher.

CIP catalogue records for this book are available from the British Library and the US Library of Congress

ISBN 1-84112-313-7

Printed and bound in Great Britain

This book is printed on acid-free paper

Substantial discounts on bulk quantities of Capstone books are available to corporations, professional associations and other organizations. Please contact Capstone for more details on +44 (0)1865 798 623 or (fax) +44 (0)1865 240 941 or (e-mail) info@wiley-capstone.co.uk

Contents

Introduction to ExpressExec

ExpressExec is 3 million words of the latest management thinking compiled into 10 modules. Each module contains 10 individual titles forming a comprehensive resource of current business practice written by leading practitioners in their field. From brand management to balanced scorecard, ExpressExec enables you to grasp the key concepts behind each subject and implement the theory immediately. Each of the 100 titles is available in print and electronic formats.

Through the ExpressExec.com Website you will discover that you can access the complete resource in a number of ways:

» printed books or e-books;
» e-content – PDF or XML (for licensed syndication) adding value to an intranet or Internet site;
» a corporate e-learning/knowledge management solution providing a cost-effective platform for developing skills and sharing knowledge within an organization;
» bespoke delivery – tailored solutions to solve your need.

Why not visit www.expressexec.com and register for free key management briefings, a monthly newsletter and interactive skills checklists. Share your ideas about ExpressExec and your thoughts about business today.

Please contact elound@wiley-capstone.co.uk for more information.

Introduction to Managing Intellectual Property

What is intellectual property (IP) and why is it important? This chapter provides an overview of the key issues, explains the growing significance of effective management of IP, and includes:

» the link with intellectual capital; and
» challenges in managing IP.

"If HP knew what HP knows, we would be three times as profitable."

Lewis Platt, chairman, Hewlett-Packard

WHAT INTELLECTUAL PROPERTY IS

"Intellectual property" – "IPR", or more commonly, "IP" – covers a range of different instruments that can be used to define, protect and exploit new ideas that an individual, or a company, has created. These range from the most well-known – patents–through to probably the hardest to define, know-how. At a high level the types of intellectual property rights that exist and their key applications are:

» patents: protection for inventions;
» copyright: protection for creative output whether words, music, media or art;
» trademarks: protection for signs which distinguish products or services;
» design rights: protection for external appearances of products; and
» know-how: internal knowledge that is kept within the organization.

Today these are increasingly recognized not only as assets that underpin corporate competitiveness in terms of providing barriers, but also as assets that can be traded, can create new opportunities, and most significantly, if managed correctly, can create value. Unlike many other fixed assets that can only be bought and sold, IP has multiple uses. Being at heart information, it can easily be moved around, can be added to and divided, and most importantly, through the licensing avenue, the same piece of IP can be sold numerous times.

WHY INTELLECTUAL PROPERTY IS IMPORTANT

Intellectual property is an area that has grown significantly in importance and relevance over the past century. It was originally introduced in the fifteenth century as a means of providing a monopoly for production; today it is recognized not only as a mechanism for protection but for creating value that sits at the forefront of corporate strategy. Companies like IBM use their IP to generate nearly 10% of their annual revenue from licensing; and stars like ARM and Qualcomm can achieve nearer 100%.

In the media industry, protected TV formats such as *Big Brother*, *Survivor*, *The Weakest Link* and the *Teletubbies* create massive revenues for their originators. New forms of IP are being created, patents are being granted for gene sequences, Internet business methods and even software. Companies are now aggressively policing and protecting their IP as shown by a series of high-profile court cases involving Kodak, Microsoft, Amazon and Napster. All these changes prove that for organizations large and small, IP management must become a core capability which their executives will need to master if they are to compete effectively in the twenty-first century and beyond.

THE LINK WITH INTELLECTUAL CAPITAL

In the knowledge economy, information is king. As ideas, brands and logos have become more valuable than traditional assets such as infrastructure, buildings and machines, the concept of intellectual capital has, in the past decade, gained significant momentum and increased its presence in the boardroom. Underpinned by the recognition that it is what an organization knows that is the key driver of competitive advantage in the twenty-first century, led by the likes of Skandia, the Swedish financial services company, firms have begun to focus more on how they can increase their intellectual capital in both its component areas: structural capital – the value that exists within the organization, its customer base, and its brand; and human capital – the value that can be associated with its people. Whereas structural capital is therefore something that largely remains within the organization, human capital is clearly transitory, lasting only as long as an employee remains an employee.

In either case, capturing and exploiting the intellectual capital within the firm is clearly a major challenge, and in partnership with initiatives such as knowledge management, intellectual property, its creation, its management and its exploitation is a key mechanism for achieving this. Whether a consultancy, software producer, TV company, fashion house or PC manufacturer, firms across multiple sectors now have to manage better their IP as a key component of their corporate strategy.

MANAGING IP

Although many find the management of IP too academic, too legal or too abstract a subject, all firms have to learn how to use IP and recognize that it can be efficiently managed to create and enhance the competitive edge of an organization. It may appear a complex issue. In reality it is fairly straightforward. It may seem to be something that applies to only a few sectors. Actually it applies to all. Lastly, you may think that it is a challenge for the future. This is not the case. Managing intellectual property is a capability that you need to build today. This book provides a guide to the subject and its implications and manifestations that will help you understand why and how you can improve your organization's ability to capitalize on the opportunities that are there for you to grasp.

What Managing Intellectual Property Is

Is managing IP simply filing patent applications or is there something else? This chapter explains all five core types of intellectual property rights and details the three key components of managing IP:

» recording
» analyzing
» exploiting.

Managing your IP is all about exploiting the knowledge that you own. This may be knowledge that has been converted into tangible assets such as patents. It may be knowledge that you are aware of; it may be knowledge that is hidden. It may be intangible assets such as your brand, or even know-how that exists within your organization. Whichever, these varied types of knowledge can all be seen as intellectual property and, as such, are something that can be used to create or destroy value. This chapter explains what is involved in managing your IP.

The first step is to gain a better understanding of five core types of IP which can exist within the firm and how they are created.

PATENTS (UK) OR UTILITY PATENTS (US)

Patents were created to prevent inventions from being copied or repeated. In return for inventors disclosing their developments they are awarded legal protection to prevent others "producing, using or selling their invention without their permission" in all those geographic areas where it has been granted. A patent also prevents anyone importing anything that may infringe it. Each patent normally has a limited lifetime of 20 years, though this can be extended to 25 years when the granting of the patent is delayed due to consideration of issues such as national security.

The invention that is being patented may be a "process," a "machine," a "manufacture" or a "composition of matter." A process covers both a core process and an act or method such as an industrial or technical process; manufacture covers all manufactured items; and composition of matter describes chemical compositions of existing or new materials. A prerequisite for a patent to be granted is that the invention has to have some functional or technical aspect, which is an improvement on an existing technology. The US leads the debate on what can and cannot be patented, and has created a number of exceptions to patentability such as abstract ideas, laws of nature and natural phenomena.

A patent application consists of a description along with a set of illustrative drawings. At the end is a series of numbered paragraphs called the "claims," that define the scope of the invention and which a patent office assesses by determining if there was any relevant technology existing prior to the filing of the patent which could prevent it being a novel step. When originally filed by the inventor, a patent is given a "priority date." If a similar invention is found which was created before this date then it is termed "prior art" and can invalidate the patent application as someone else had already made the invention. Any similar inventions created after this priority date would then infringe the patent if it were granted.

Before submitting a full application, an inventor can make a provisional application to gain an earlier priority date. There is then a twelve-month period within which to file the full application for the same invention and claim the same priority date. Once filed, a patent office will search for similar patents and if any are found, it will notify the inventor so giving an opportunity to make a rebuttal and explain why the claimed invention is novel and does not infringe the existing patents. Normally this process takes at least 18 months, and filing a full patent normally takes two-and-a-half years from a provisional application.

If the patent is to be extended beyond the inventor's domestic market, the application is made for wider protection through the Patent Co-operation Treaty (PCT) (explained in Chapter 5). This allows the same application to be made for more than one country at a time.

Once a patent has been granted, the invention can be licensed. In effect this is hiring the patent to another party, allowing the organization to exploit it, in return for an agreed fee. In addition to licensing, patents can also be assigned or sold. Though the inventor is still named on the patent, the buyer becomes the named owner.

COPYRIGHT

Copyright prevents another party copying content that has been created and then "fixed" in some manner. Fixing can be through having it written down, recorded, filmed or captured in the form of electronic data. The idea becomes locked in the physical world.

Unlike patents, copyright does not need to be applied for as it is automatically created and established as soon as the material is fixed. Examples of copyrighted material are literary works, computer programs, paintings, photos, songs, films, TV programs and newspaper articles.

TRADEMARKS (UK) OR MARKS (US)

Trademarks are defined by The Patent Office (UK) as "any sign that can distinguish the products or services" and by the US Patent and Trademark Office (USPTO) as "a word, name, symbol or device that is used in trade with goods to indicate the source of the goods and to distinguish them from the goods of others."

Other types of trademarks include service marks, distinguishing a service as opposed to a product; certification marks that certify the origin of a good; and collective marks that indicate that the company producing the product belongs to a certain union or organization.

Once registered with a patent office, a trademark prevents someone providing the same goods or services under the same trademark, but not under a different trademark. In essence, it tries to protect the identity a firm may have given their product in order to distinguish it from similar competing ones. This can cover both the name and the logo. The criteria for acceptance are that it must be distinctive, legal, and different from existing trademarks.

Internet domain names can also be registered with the USPTO, though only where the name is in line with a trademark. For example, where the company name is ABC.com, this could be registered as a trademark, but it also happens to be a URL, and where the company name is ABC, the ABC.com could not be registered as all this does is indicate the location of its Website.

DESIGN MARKS (UK) OR DESIGN PATENTS (US)

Design marks or design patents are monopoly rights to the outward appearance of an object – for example a chair, a pen, a building, or a car. What distinguishes these from the utility patent is that they cover the way an object looks, whereas the latter covers the way it works.

Design marks are registered in a similar way to patents, but there is only one claim – to the appearance. Like patents, design marks can be sold or licensed.

KNOW-HOW

The last form of IP, and perhaps the hardest to define, is "know-how." It can be described as an individual's or a company's knowledge.

Frequently it is not written down, but when applied, can give rise to patents, copyright, trademarks or design marks. The core means of protecting know-how is through confidentiality agreements, and specific clauses in employment contracts preventing disclosure of company information. Examples range from Microsoft's source code and Coca-Cola's ingredients, to investments banks' "algorithms for derivatives" pricing strategy, accountants' procedures, and approaches to tax compliance. Know-how can be the most effective form of IP as it prevents competitors understanding your expertise and thus utilizing it for their advantage. However, as it is never formally registered with any legal body, it can disappear with a single leak or one disgruntled ex-employee.

With this understanding of the five different types of intellectual property that can exist and how they can be created, we can now consider what is involved in managing a portfolio of IP, and understand how to realize the maximum value from it.

WHAT IS INVOLVED IN MANAGING IP

Managing IP should be part of a company's strategy, part of its organizational structure, a core capability – not a task delegated to patent agents and attorneys. Management is distinct from maintenance. Managing IP is a responsibility of the organization; maintaining it, whether in terms of drafting, filing or updating applications, is the responsibility of patent agents and attorneys who are most commonly external to the organization. In this new approach, managing IP is elevated to a commercial concern.

Many high technology companies have now created patent management departments or divisions to manage their portfolios and extract the maximum value from them. For example, IBM set up the IBM Technology Group (ITG) in the late 1990s that, through proper management, has been able to generate over $1bn in revenues from the organization's 10,000 patents. Similarly Xerox formed Xerox New Enterprises to develop and market its 8,000 patents, a move analysts believe will create over $24bn in new wealth for the company's shareholders if it generates only half the revenue per patent that IBM earns. Moreover, this revenue is almost all translated into pure profit as the costs associated with the creation of the IP in the first place have already been absorbed.

For firms that have evolved to generate value from their IP, managing IP has three core components:

» recording the IP the company owns;
» analyzing the value of this IP; and
» exploiting the IP to maximize revenue.

RECORDING THE IP

Although not 100% guaranteed, most organizations have some record of the IP that they own. Whether this exists in an easily accessible database, or is distributed across multiple geographies or business units is another matter. The key challenge that many companies face is in collating the basic information into a single coherent database that provides users with an understanding of what type of IP exists, when it was created, what it covers, and where it has been used. The database should be able to be mined to see whether old patents might apply to new applications. Although relatively simple in theory, many companies do not even have this basic component in place. However, when they do bring it into being, it is not uncommon for surprises to surface. Take for example BT which, when it created and mined its database of 14,000 patents, found US patent number 4873662 granted in 1989. The company claims that this gives it the exclusive rights to the hyperlinks used in the www. Currently BT is suing the US ISP Prodigy for infringement.

ANALYZING THE IP

The next step is to understand the organizational value of each piece of IP. Notice that we distinguish between *organizational* value and *inherent* value. To illustrate this, imagine two patents have the same inherent value of $1mn in future licensing revenue, but patent A can be exploited in the market in which the company already exists, whereas patent B would mean the company entering a new market. Patent A has a greater organizational value than patent B.

Having undertaken a (manual!) IP audit of its 30,000 patents, Dow Chemicals assigned each piece of IP to the most applicable business unit. The level at which this can be done clearly varies across different organizations – some assign to companies, some to business units and some to departments. In essence this is a balance between working at a meaningful level and at one that is too detailed and will make any analysis too difficult to complete.

To estimate the potential of each piece of IP, Dow created an IP audit grid.

» Along the vertical axis it plotted the growth of each geographic business unit relative to the GDP for the country in which it was based. This allowed the organization to compare it to the "average" growth of the local economy. (If specific markets rather than countries align a company's business units, it is more appropriate to use the growth of that market rather than GDP.)
» Across the horizontal axis Dow then plotted a subjective assessment as to whether each patent would be used in future plans or not. This was divided into three categories: Current Plans, Future Plans or Not in Plans.

The resulting analysis (see Fig. 2.1) provided clear segregation of the organization's patent portfolio and how the constituent patents should be exploited.

The company then managed its patents according to their position.

» Those towards the top left hand corner are the most valuable, as they have the highest potential growth and are part of the company's current plans. These are maintained.
» Those in the top right hand corner are seen as valuable but as they are not part of the company's current or future plans, the best way to extract value from them is to license them out to a third party.
» Those in the bottom right hand corner are abandoned as they are neither in the company's future plans, nor likely to be a source of future growth.

The result of this approach for Dow was significant. Through pruning its portfolio and licensing non-core patents the company saved millions in taxes and unnecessary patent maintenance fees, and boosted its bottom line by over $100mn.

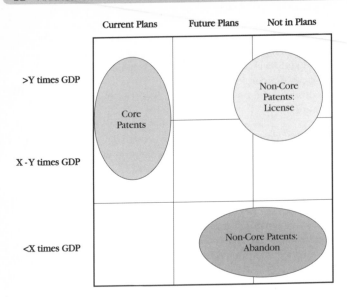

Fig. 2.1 Dow IP analysis.

EXPLOITING THE IP

As can be seen from the example above, significant revenue can be generated from exploiting the right IP. Whilst internal value can be maintained by using core patents in a defensive capacity to defend existing areas of operation, external value can be created through licensing or selling. In considering the license option, here are some of the key criteria.

» Defined fields – for what applications will you allow the licensee to exploit your invention in? The same patent can be used in different fields to create more than one revenue stream.
» Exclusivity – will you agree to license to only a single third party, in order to give them a head start in their market? Normally, a licensee would pay more for this privilege.
» Duration – how long is the licensing agreement for?

» Advance – a great threat when licensing to a competitor who is to become your customer, is that the competitor may license the patent and then do nothing with it. To prevent this, an advance or upfront fee can be charged as a form of commitment. As well as this, it is normal to include a term stating that if the invention is not exploited within a certain timeframe, the agreement is cancelled.

By exploiting its IP properly, a company should be able to move from using patents, trademarks and other instruments as merely a defensive, blocking measure, to using them as a valuable source of future revenue.

KEY INSIGHTS

» The five forms of intellectual property are patents, copyright, trademarks, design marks and know-how.
» Patents prevent inventions from being copied or repeated.
» Copyright protects content when it is written down, recorded or captured electronically.
» Trademarks provide protection for signs that distinguish products and services.
» Design marks protect the external appearance of an object.
» Know-how is the alternative to public disclosure and relies on maintaining secrecy.
» Patents, trademarks and design marks have to be applied for and granted.
» Copyright is automatically granted and does not therefore require application.
» Managing IP should be part of a company's strategy and organizational structure.
» IP management has three core components – recording, analyzing and exploiting.
» Organizations should maintain a coherent record of their IP, ideally in a database.
» The value of each piece of IP has to be understood.
» Internal value comes from the defensive use of IP.
» External value comes from licensing or selling IP.

Evolution of Intellectual Property

How did intellectual property develop? What have been the key changes? What are the current issues? Chapter 3 explores the evolution of the topic from the fifteenth century to today, and covers:

» the growth of patenting in the eighteenth and nineteenth centuries;
» key twentieth-century developments;
» copyright's increasingly significant role;
» the trademark's emergence as a distinguishing component of IP;
» design rights growth in the UK; and
» current issues for managing IP.

Intellectual property has mixed origins: patents can be traced back to the fifteenth century; copyright to 1662; design right to the end of the eighteenth century; and trademarks to 1875. However, these are all dates when these varied forms of IP first existed in a legal and hence executable sense. It was the scholars of ancient Greece and the Roman Empire who were the first to be concerned about who should be recognized as authors of work, but at the time this was purely from the perspective of intellectual ownership and acknowledgment of creativity rather than any economic rights.

In terms of protection of invention, and the ability to secure revenue from the ownership of intellectual property, developments in a number of fields brought IP into being as a legal entity. For patents it was the move by the English Crown to provide specific grants of privilege to favored manufacturers and traders which kicked off activity. For copyright it was the advent of printing that eventually promoted formalization of intellectual property for the evolving industry. For design right it was the growth of textile production that prompted associated protection. Finally for trademarks, it was the idea of differentiation between distinctive providers of a trade or service, and the associated goodwill that existed, that first gave birth to the concept of protection in this field. Over the five centuries since patents started the IP bandwagon rolling, to today, when protection of business methods, software, genes and Internet images are driving IP to the forefront of many organizations' thinking and growth strategies, there has been a massive change in the perception and context of what IP is and how to manage it.

THE EVOLUTION OF PATENTS

The city council of Florence awarded the first recorded patent, or letters patent, in 1421 for the production of glass. This was the first of several patents granted in order to provide specific privileges in the fifteenth century in the small states of Northern Italy. The first patent in England was granted by Henry VI in 1449 to John of Utynam and marked the beginning of a number of 20-year monopolies. This was also for a method of making glass; this time, stained glass required for the windows of Eton College, by a technique that had not previously been known in England. It was however during the reigns of the Tudors and

Stuarts that the granting of patents became more common. During the 30 years from 1561 to 1590 Elizabeth I granted about 50 patents that provided monopolies for the manufacture and sales of such items as soap, leather, salt, glass, sailcloth, and paper.

Although some patents were refused on the grounds of propriety – for example, an application in 1596 for a design of water closet – the granting of monopolies became increasingly open to abuse as grants for items such as knives were made in return for favors, generating significant revenue streams for monarchs and politicians. By 1610, as criticism from the judiciary and the public increased, James I was forced to revoke all patents and declare that "monopolies are things contrary to the law." The subsequent Statute of Monopolies of 1624 clarified the issue by rendering illegal all monopolies except those granted to inventors of "a new manner of manufacture" for a period of 14 years. No longer could patents be awarded to suit the needs of the nation's leaders.

With this in place, the patent system gradually evolved through the courts and the work of lawyers and judges, but without further government regulation. In 1718, James Puckle's patent for a machine gun was rejected on the basis that it did not contain a "specification" – a recently introduced requirement for a detailed written description of the nature of an invention, established in the reign of Queen Anne. Similarly Richard Arkwright's famous patent for spinning machines was voided in 1785, 10 years after its invention. However, James Watt's patent for steam engines in 1796 established the precedent that a patent could be granted for an improvement to a known machine and not just a wholly new invention.

Outside Britain patents began to take hold as a means of protecting inventions, often, as with the first patent issued in America in 1641, granted by colonial governments. In 1787 John Fitch, one of those who claimed to have invented the steamboat, persuaded several members of the US Constitutional Convention to acknowledge the need for legislation, resulting in amendments to the Constitution on September 5 of that year to establish a US patent system. The first US Patent Act came into force in 1790 and was administered by a commission composed of the secretary of state, the secretary of war, and the attorney general. The basis of the present system was established in the US Patent Act of July 4 1836, which was later modified in 1870 and 1952.

Fuelled by the technological changes of the industrial revolution, during the nineteenth century patenting expanded significantly both in terms of quantity and reach, with every major European country establishing a formal procedure, but by the middle of the century the process had become lengthy and cumbersome. With the Great Exhibition of 1851 in London accelerating demand for reform, the Patent Law Amendment Act of 1852 completely overhauled the UK system, laying down a simplified process and establishing the world's first patent office.

In 1883 a staff of patent examiners was created to undertake examination and ensure that the specification described any invention appropriately. This, and a subsequent act in 1902, established the basis of a UK system that lasted throughout most of the twentieth century. Also in 1883, the Paris Convention for the protection of intellectual property was the first major international treaty designed to enable protection in multiple countries. Ten years later this led to the creation of the United International Bureau for the Protection of Intellectual Property, an organization that in 1970 became the World Intellectual Property Organization (WIPO) when the Patent Co-operation Treaty (PCT) came into force. Following the Paris Convention, the first Japanese patent law was passed in 1885.

Over the following years, especially in the US, some interesting developments occurred – in particular, the Plant Patent Act of 1930 which overrode the principle that plants are products of nature and hence unpatentable. It established the ability to gain protection for new varieties of asexually reproducing plants, something widened in 1970 to sexually distinct plants, thus paving the way for the advent of patenting genetically modified products in 1980. The 1964 Plant Varieties and Seeds Act brought this increase in scope to the UK. Also in the US, the Patent Office reacted to increasing criticism of anticompetitive use of patents by large companies between the two world wars by becoming less willing to grant questionable patents.

Recent developments

The next major development in patenting was again initiated in the UK with the 1977 Patents Act. Considered to be the most radical piece of IP legislation for over a century, this set out to ensure that the system today is more suited to modern industry, sufficiently flexible to accommodate changes in technology and adapted to operate as part of a wider international context.

Since 1980 there has been a significant change in how organizations approach the management of IP, and particularly patents. In 1980 the average number of US patent applications was in the order of 100,000 per annum of which around 60,000 were granted. Twenty years later applications were running at over 270,000 with over 150,000 being granted. Especially in the last five years of the twentieth century, companies such as Sun and Microsoft dramatically increased the number of patents they were granted, from an average of 100 in 1995 to over 600 in 1999. The key motivation has been the change in perspective held in the 1960s and 1970s, from patents being seen as monopolistic barriers to creativity, where most patents contested in the courts were thrown out, to a point today where two in three cases are won.

In addition, several landmark decisions have made new areas of technology patentable. The first of these were changes in the US system in 1980 that allowed patents to be granted for genes. This caused an explosion in IP in the whole biotechnology arena and paved the way for the eventual patenting of cloning techniques by PPL Therapeutics for Dolly the sheep in 1998. This also led to the inclusion of a number of politically contentious issues related to IP protection for pharmaceutical and agricultural products in the latest round of the World Trade Organization (WTO) (see Chapter 5). In 1981, again in the US, software was seen as being patentable and hence activity in this area increased, particularly after Microsoft had to pay IBM $30mn for infringement.

Today, virtually any software program, if novel and non-obvious, is patentable in the US, although not in Europe – not that this really makes any difference in a global village dominated by the US. Lastly, and perhaps most controversially, in 1998 the US patent office determined that business models were patentable resulting in a gold rush mentality, fuelled by successful court cases for both Amazon.com and Priceline.com (see Chapter 4).

THE EVOLUTION OF COPYRIGHT

Although sometimes considered less significant than patents, copyright has had a similarly wild ride in its development. Although William

Caxton brought printing to England in 1476, making mass duplication of manuscripts possible, it was not until the 1709 Statute of Anne that copyright in books and other writings gained initial protection in England. In 1662 the Licensing Act had, in a bid to combat growing piracy, established a register of licensed books along with the requirement to deposit a copy in the British Library. However, it was the Statute of Anne that first introduced the concepts of an author being the owner of copyright and the principle of a fixed term of protection. This also increased the requirement of depositing copies to nine identified libraries across the country. In 1790, following on from the example of England, at the same time as it established its first patent law, the US also made copyright law federal "to secure for limited times to authors and inventors exclusive rights to their respective writing and discoveries."

Over the next century, as bilateral agreements between the UK and the US came into force, there were incremental amendments to copyright laws both sides of the Atlantic to cover such issues as musical performances (1833), and paintings, drawings, and photographs (1883 in the UK and 1884 in the US). It was however with the 1886 Berne Convention that the International Copyright Act first established a wider framework, abolished the requirement to deposit foreign works and introduced an exclusive right to import or produce translations, something which in 1853 had been rejected by a US court when author Harriet Beecher Stowe had claimed that a German translation of *Uncle Tom's Cabin* had infringed her copyright. The Berne Convention established an International Bureau for Copyright that was integrated into the United International Bureau for the Protection of Intellectual Property in 1893.

During the early years of the twentieth century further advances included the Berlin Act of 1908 which set the duration of copyright as the life of the author plus 50 years; the US Copyright Act of 1909 which broadened the scope to cover all works of authorship; and the UK Copyright Act of 1911 which abolished protection for unpublished works except paintings and drawings. Then, in 1928, the Rome Act gave artists the right to object to the modification or destruction of a work in a way that may damage the artist's reputation. The 1956 UK Copyright Act included new technological advances including films and broadcasts. In 1971, the US decided that musical recordings and not just the compositions themselves should be shielded, and in 1976 the US Copyright Act covered photocopying of material from libraries, including for classroom use.

Recent developments

It is however, as with patents, since 1980 that major changes in what copyright covers have occurred. Beginning with software itself in 1981 and its circulation in 1990, copyright has also been extended to architectural works (1990), the telephone directory (1991), photocopying of journals (1992), downloading of *Playboy* images from the Internet (1993) and, in 1996, databases. In 1994 rap music was considered fair commercial use of an original song but, in 1999, downloading MP3 files from the Internet was ruled illegal (see Chapter 4). Recent updates to copyright laws in the UK and the US are, together with the 1996 TRIPS agreement (see Chapter 5), seeking to accommodate the increasingly diverse range of potentially protectable works, but as at the time of writing, especially with the advance of digital copyright and the Internet, the development of copyright law looks set to continue apace for many years to come.

THE EVOLUTION OF TRADEMARKS

In contrast to patents and copyright, trademarks have a relatively recent history. Although the marking of goods, including distinguishing them from those of other traders, goes back to ancient times, and rules governing the use of such marks for swords and pottery date from medieval craft guilds, it was only in the nineteenth century that the idea of trademarks developed. It was then that, used to distinguish a particular trader's goods and hence something that attracts goodwill, trademarks first became seen as a type of property. Again initiated in the UK, the Trade Marks Registration Act of 1875 established a register of marks and the Trade Marks Registry opened in London the following year. This allowed for the registration of a word, logo or picture and defined its owner, thus giving the owner the exclusive right to use it and preventing unauthorized use. Although simple, this act effectively established a procedure that has remained in place ever since. Although there have been amendments in the UK in 1883, 1905, 1938 and 1988, the law was largely unchanged until 1994. Likewise, in the US, the 1870 Trademark Act defined the standard and the 1946 Lanham Act subsequently allowed for users to establish "nationwide constructive use" of their marks.

More focused on application than legislation, trademarks have grown in relevance over the last 80 years. The rise of advertising in the 1920s was the watershed. Manufacturers and retailers, particularly in the US, fuelled a surge as brands proliferated and they relied upon rapid product style changes to stimulate customer demand. Ford, for example, spent $2mn on advertising the Model T in a single week – all focused on, and underpinned by, the Ford trademark. McDonalds, Coca-Cola and Levis paved the way. By the late twentieth century and with the 1994 UK Trade Mark Act coming into place, protection covered such things as the uniforms of the TWA air stewardesses and tag lines like Gillette's "The best a man can get." The range and scope of trademark law had increased considerably.

HISTORY OF DESIGN RIGHT

From the start of the US patent system in 1790, three different kinds of patent have been covered by the evolving legislation. These are utility patents, plant patents and design patents where the latter protect the appearance of ornamental features from being copied. However, in the UK, protection of design right has been treated separately from patents and a parallel system has duly developed.

The 1787 Design and Prints of Linen Act initiated the first specific protection for industrial designs in the UK. This "design right" gave an initial limited copyright protection for linen, cotton and muslin textile to designers and printers providing sole rights for a period of two months, a period extended by a further month in 1794. 1839 saw the next step with the Copyright and Design Act which increased protection from cotton, linen and muslin textiles to those made of wool, silk and hair and, perhaps more significant in the long term, for ornamental decoration of any manufactured article. This essentially created protection for the visual aspects of all production items. In addition, the same act also introduced a system of registration.

The 1842 Design Act consolidated coverage and the following year this was amended to cover functional, as well as ornamental features. This remained in place largely unchanged, including a period of combination with patent law between 1907 and 1946, until in 1949 the Registered Design Act amended the definition and scope of a design. This has remained in place ever since but as amended by the Copyright, Designs and Patents Act of 1988. Future amendments and changes will be necessary as the UK moves nearer to harmonization of national systems of registered design protection.

MANAGING INTELLECTUAL PROPERTY TODAY

Across all types of IP there is clearly an accelerating pace of change in both scope and application. The ability to patent business methods, gene sequences and computer software is, together with the global implications of the recent TRIPS agreement (see Chapter 5) having a profound effect on what organizations are, by and large, successfully seeking to protect and exploit. As discussed in Chapter 4, copyright of software, books and particularly music in the Internet age has come under the spotlight, especially through the cases of MP3 and Napster. In addition an increasingly aggressive stance of many corporations such as McDonalds and Nike in implementing the rights associated with their respective trademarks and design marks is also bringing these latter two into focus. Today managing your IP portfolio has become a capability requiring understanding of all the latest developments and issues across the whole IP arena and, by implication, a capability that itself will continue to evolve apace.

EVOLUTION OF INTELLECTUAL PROPERTY – TIMELINE

Table 3.1.

Table 3.1 Evolution of IP timeline.

Year	Patents	Copyright	Trade Marks/Design Rights (UK)
1421	First patent – Italy		
1449	First patent – UK		
1590	Elizabeth 1 grants 50 patents		
1624	Statute of monopolies (UK)		
1641	First patent in US (UK granted)		
1662		First Licensing Act (UK)	
1709		Statute of Anne (UK)	
1785	Arkwright's patent rejected		
1787			Design and Prints of Linen Act (UK)
1790	First US Patent Act	First US Copyright Act	
1796	Watt's patent for steam engine		
1836	Second US Patent Act		
1839		Copyright and Design Act (UK)	Copyright and Design Act (UK)
1842			Design Act (UK)
1851	Great Exhibition – London		
1852	Patent Law Amendment Act (UK)		
1853		Translation – *Uncle Tom's Cabin*	
1870			Trademark Act (US)
1875			Trade Marks Registration Act (UK)
1883	Paris Convention		

(*Continued*)

Table 3.1   (*Continued*).

Year	Patents	Copyright	Trade Marks/Design Rights (UK)
1884		Photographs covered by copyright (US)	
1885	First Patent Act (Japan)		
1886		Berne Convention	
1902	Patent Act (UK)		
1907			Design incorporated in Patents (UK)
1908		Berlin Act – 50-year life for copyright	
1909		Copyright Act (US)	
1911		Copyright Act (UK)	
1928		Rome Act	
1930	Plant Patent Act (US)		
1946			Lanham Act (US)
1949			Registered Design Act (UK)
1956		Copyright Act (UK)	
1964	Plants covered by patent (UK)		
1970	WIPO/PCT comes into being		
1971		Musical recordings covered (US)	
1976		Copyright Act (US)	
1977	Patents Act (UK)		
1980	Genes and GM foods covered		
1981	Software patentable (US)	Computer software covered	
1988			Copyright, Designs and Patents Act (UK)

(*Continued overleaf*)

Table 3.1 (*Continued*).

Year	Patents	Copyright	Trade Marks/Design Rights (UK)
1990		Circulation of software (US)	
1990		Architectural works (US)	
1991		Telephone directory covered	
1993		*Playboy* - Internet images	
1994		Rap music allowed to sample	Trade Mark Act (UK)
1995		US amendments	
1996		Databases covered/TRIPS	
1998	Dolly the sheep - cloning patent		
1998	Business methods patentable (US)		
2000		Napster and MP3 prosecuted by RIAA	

KEY INSIGHTS

» Intellectual property dates back to the fifteenth century.
» The first patent was awarded by the City of Florence in 1421.
» Patenting grew significantly across Europe and the US during the nineteenth century.
» In the past 20 years, there has been rapid development of what can be patented.
» Copyright first gave protection to authors in 1709.
» The 1886 Berne Convention established an international framework for copyright.

» Since 1980 there has been significant widening of scope for copyright.
» Trademarks first appeared in the nineteenth century.
» Design rights came into force in the late eighteenth century.
» Today IP is changing faster than ever before in both scope and reach.

The E-Dimension

What effect has the Internet had on managing intellectual property? Who have been the winners and the losers? This chapter reviews the impacts and focuses on three core issues with a major case study of Napster:

» bypassing IP;
» defending existing IP; and
» creating new IP.

The arrival of the Internet has, in many areas, had a dramatic and in some respects revolutionary impact on IP. For some, particularly individuals and groups who see the Internet as a way of bypassing traditional multinational corporate control of IP, the apparent benefits that have been enabled from the development of, for example, Linux, have been enormous. For others, especially copyright owners and exploiters like software developers, publishers and the music industry, the Internet has conversely provided arguably the biggest challenge to their continued profitability that they have so far encountered. Still, for others like Amazon and E-Bay who are seen as the early winners in the e-world, protecting and managing their IP have been core mechanisms in securing their business models and thereby enabling them to maintain a competitive advantage over their many emulators.

In essence, the Internet has brought into focus three core issues which influence the opportunity for managing IP, and also the means of doing so:

» bypassing IP;
» defending existing IP; and
» creating new IP.

BYPASSING IP

In the early days of software development, programmers were open to sharing all aspects of their work in order to enable each other to make and share improvements as they went along. As the computing industry evolved in the 1970s with the advent of large-scale corporate ownership and several companies, most significantly Microsoft, coming to the fore, organizations began to hold back and keep the source code for their operating systems, their core IP, hidden. This made the software proprietary and thus turned it into big business. Pure programmers were against this from the start as it meant that a few core companies could maintain control of the emerging standard operating systems and thereby control the industry.

Although clearly an advantage for Microsoft and certain companies whose market value multiplied exponentially as the intellectual capital associated with the proprietary know-how behind the varied applications became ever more critical to their competitive position, for others the inability to access and share core information was a major concern. As a reaction to the increasing impact of copyright on the software industry, in 1983 Richard Stillman founded the Free Software Foundation, and developed the concept of "copyleft" that he codified into a license, the General Public License, which now comes with most open source software.

The Internet has on the other hand enabled a new mass-sharing, quick communication system that is perfect for the open source movement which advocates free and open access to core software. The network effect potentially renders the corporate control systems allied to secrecy vulnerable to easy development with transparent decision-making and minimal bureaucracy. Software could now arguably emerge, driven by quality and performance and not by corporate ambition. Although slow at first, with a few isolated programs being developed co-operatively, the explosion of freeware and shareware in the early 1990s was driven by programmers for whom the highest achievement is not financial gain, but writing a "patch" that passes peer review and is incorporated into the next release. The core essence is that there is no intellectual property to be owned, as it is free to all and the whole IP system is therefore effectively bypassed.

The major software organizations were aware, concerned, but mostly tolerant of minor activities in the open source arena until the late 1990s when Linux took off. It was created in 1991 when Linus Torvalds realized that, in a bid to make a free operating system that would be good enough for use in large corporate networks he needed to be able to access the very best, and invited people across the Internet to write the varied modules of what has become a real rival to Windows and Unix. In 2000, 27% of total shipments of server operating systems were Linux-based compared with 41% for Windows. The scale of this achievement is even more significant when one considers that, through the open source approach, Linux has been created with no profit motive, a perspective so totally at odds with contemporary business culture.

Dell, Compaq, HP and significantly IBM, the old enemy of the original hackers, have all invested heavily in Linux as they want it to become the computing standard so that their respective e-business solutions can all be easily integrated. Microsoft, as the key corporate most threatened by Linux, is fighting back claiming that open source software restricts innovation and undermines commerce, fundamentally through bypassing IP. Which of the two alternate perspectives will prevail is for time to tell; however, fuelled by the Internet, the advent of Linux and other open source programs such as Sun Microsystems' OpenOffice do seem to be gaining more and more momentum.

DEFENDING EXISTING IP

Perhaps the most visible impact of the Internet on how organizations manage their IP has been associated with the threats that the Internet has brought into place. Particularly relevant to copyright, how organizations have tried, succeeded and failed to defend their IP in cyberspace has been one of the most prominent IP issues over the past few years. The three core areas of impact for this have been in the software, music and, to a lesser extent, book publishing industries.

Software

Although not uniquely driven by the Internet, software piracy has undeniably been made both more pervasive and more accessible through the medium. On behalf of software companies, organizations such as the Business Software Alliance have been fighting against increased piracy in both traditional and Internet form. On the basis of lost revenue to the companies involved and associated impact on the economies of particularly the US and the UK, the organization is involved in a continuous series of legal actions focused on defending the IP position of its members.

Whilst world piracy rates associated with unauthorized duplication of software have fallen from 45% in 1995 to 37% in 2000, at an estimated $11.75bn per annum in lost revenue, it is still a major problem, traditionally most prevalent in Vietnam (97% piracy rate in 2000), China (94%), Indonesia (89%), Russia (88%), and Pakistan (83%). However the increased reach of the Internet and the ability easily to download all types of software has led to an increase in software piracy in the West where revenue impact is more severe. 2000 losses in revenue of $3bn in both Western Europe and the US indicate an increase from comparatively low traditional piracy rates, of 40% and

25% respectively, upwards as nearly one-third of all software sales are conducted via e-commerce. Prevention at this level of Internet-driven piracy is however a major problem for the authorities, not only because it is far more difficult to restrict than the traditional approach of shutting down illegal product facilities but also because, as represented by the advent of Linux mentioned above, there is little popular support for some of the larger companies such as Microsoft, and the open source movement is clearly directly opposed to protecting software copyright.

Music

Certainly one of the most public IP fights of recent times has been between MP3.com and Napster and the might of the world music industries, as the former have striven to enable easier access to the catalogues of the latter via the Internet. Summarized in the case study below, this three-year struggle has highlighted the issue of copyright ownership and brought it into the limelight for a wider audience.

Books

Although initially feared that it might cause as much an erosion of royalties as happened in the music industry, by comparison the publishing industry has not suffered the same level of impact and has not had to defend its IP to the same extent. With the exception of a few high profile authors such as Stephen King, far fewer than expected have chosen to bypass the traditional publishing industry value chain and author direct to the Internet. Ironically, given the ease with which a word document or pdf file can be posted, downloaded and read, abuse of IP of copyright in the written form has been less extensive than in the cases of music and software. Partly because of the lower value of each item and therefore the smaller margin to be saved by direct access, but also because of the extent to which the publishing industry has actually adapted and embraced the Internet as a promotion and sales channel, the impact has been far less damaging.

E-mails and copyright

Within this topic, a few words on e-mail are also worthwhile. Although e-mails and Websites may have copyright protection, the rights are subject to limitations. Copyright protects only the specific expression and not the ideas conveyed or facts contained. Later works that happen to be similar to an earlier message or Web page do not infringe copyright if they are independently created. Whilst Web pages and e-mail messages are in principle protected by copyright as soon as they are created, copyright registration is required before their owners can bring suit, and early registration helps to provide options that make lawsuits enforceable.

Unlike books and other published materials, Web pages are however frequently updated and hence, in the extreme, separate registration of copyright would be required for each update. Many organizations choose simply to provide notice of copyright at the end of each page in the hope that this will deter rather than prevent copying. Litigation is expensive and hence largely avoided; however if people choose this path then the two key questions to be answered in advance are whether use of another's work is likely to offend, and are the benefits worth the bother and cost to resolve any dispute.

CREATING NEW IP

The patenting of business methods is, despite its currency and relevance to the Internet, not a new issue. Companies have, for example, protected the way they sell airline tickets and how they manage money-market accounts. However, it is the growth of the Internet that has accelerated focus on this area, particularly as the so-called business model became the source of so much attention in the major growth years of 1998 to 2000.

The fundamental element, as far as the IP authorities are concerned, is the difference between a business model and a business method. The former is seen as a strategy or a vision, whereas the business method is a specific way of doing business; and hence potentially, this is what can be protected. In 1999, 600 patents were issued by the US patent office related to software-enabled business methods. This rose to over 1000 the following year.

By far the most significant patented business methods, in terms of publicity gained from their protection, have been those gained by Amazon.com and Priceline.com, both of which have been deployed as a competitive weapon. In the case of Amazon it was the company's patent on its "one-click" system for processing customer orders that has been the focus. Faced with increasing imitation from other Internet retailers, Amazon filed an infringement suit against Barnes & Noble, its bricks and mortar competitor and its Express Lane process. Although arguably a small element in the overall offering, along with its patent for click-through affiliate relationships, the protection granted to Amazon on the one-click component of its business has been a key driver in enabling it to see off not only Barnes & Noble but also other imitators such as bol.com in its continued lead at the forefront of the e-commerce space.

Similarly, Priceline.com has also used its "name your own price" reverse auction as a competitive weapon, suing Microsoft and claiming infringement of its patent for buyer-driven commerce systems. Although both companies had discussed possible joint ventures – and, to make things more complex, Priceline's vice chairman moved to Microsoft – no agreement was ever finalized before Microsoft launched its Hotel Price Matcher service on Expedia, and thus Jay Walker, founder of Priceline, took Microsoft to court. Interestingly, Priceline is based on just one of multiple patents for business methods created by Walker and his so-called "patent factory" Walker Digital, which he likes to compare to Edison's Menlo Park laboratory.

Another example of successful leverage of IP created specifically because of the Internet is the search engine Google. Launched in 1998 by Sergey Brin and Larry Page, two Stanford students, Google quickly developed a cult reputation as the fastest and most accurate search engine in cyberspace. By April 2001, it had pushed aside earlier and more heavily marketed competitors such as Ask Jeeves, AltaVista and Infoseek to become the most popular search engine in the US with an index of 1.3 billion entries compiled by the company's 10,000 computers picking 1000 pages a second.

Named after the googol, the mathematical term for the number one followed by 100 zeros, and including 50 PhDs in its 220 staff – whereas other search engines use the principle that relevance is based on repetition – Google measures a page's pertinence according to whether other sites, especially popular ones like Amazon, have already linked to it. Also, unlike the early entrants into this arena, Google has not relied solely on revenue from advertising but has also licensed its proprietary

IP to other Websites, portals and WAP providers including Netscape, Yahoo! in the US and Vodafone and Virgin in the UK. Typically charging $1mn license fees per company, revenues are forecast to reach $50mn by early 2002 and a potential value at IPO of up to $250mn.

Finally, another prominent new area for IP management created by the advent of the Internet has been the registration and ownership of domain names. Clearly closely linked to either existing brands seeking Internet presence (pepsi.com, mcdonalds.com, sony.com, cnn.com etc) or new ventures created through using the Internet as a medium (amazon.com, e-bay.com, yahoo.com, beeb.com, etc.) domain names have become a natural extension of trademarks and service-marks in requiring effective management as part of an organization's IP portfolio.

However, in their scope and the potential access afforded to them, domain names have also taken on a life of their own in the value that has been associated with the ownership of the associated IP. Examples such as buy.com, sex.com, soccer.com, and fly.com have all been seen to have intrinsic value in the varied areas of potential application and use. Although the fallout following the dot.com boom has reduced some of the valuations from peaks of $10mn for some of these and their like, the significance of ownership and exploitation of domain names as part of the IP portfolio is nevertheless still a core issue for many organizations with an e-commerce or e-business stance to promote and protect.

MP3, NAPSTER AND IP IN THE MUSIC INDUSTRY

Context

In the mid 1990s, before the rapid explosion of the Internet, the major concern for the global music industry was how to prevent counterfeiting. Music piracy worldwide meant that the five major labels – Sony, EMI, Warner, BMG, and Universal – were collectively losing up to $1bn per annum in lost revenue from royalties. Although at the time largely based in Taiwan, China and Hong Kong, manufacture of counterfeit cassettes and increasingly more significantly, compact discs, was the growing global problem that both the labels and the industry groups such as the IFPI (International Federation of Phonographic

Industries) and the RIAA (Recording Industry Association of America) were all seeking to overcome. This was being achieved both by direct legal action against pirates, aimed at shutting down production facilities, and through introducing overt, covert and forensic technologies into the products to help detect and prevent counterfeiting.

With the arrival of MP3 technology in 1997 and the creation of Napster in 1999, the priorities for the music industry changed dramatically. Coupled with the emergence of CD-R technology, the ability for mass downloading of tracks from the Internet was suddenly even more significant than the existing CD piracy problem. Anyone could now access any piece of music from anywhere in the world, download to their PC or MP3 player and even burn their own CD, totally bypassing the existing industry value chain. Royalties, the lifeblood of the music industry and hence the core mechanism for generating revenue from the associated IP, were all now potentially on the verge of being lost.

Since then, as the music industry has nearly lost and then fought back to regain influence, if not full control, of music distribution the pace of events has been dramatic. Somewhat slowly at first, the music industry has used the same two elements of litigation and the introduction of new technologies to stand up to the threat. The summary of events below shows just how significant the efforts deployed by the industry have been, and how strongly it has used every option open to it to defend its IP position and protect the vital royalty revenues.

The IP battle

Following the foundation of MP3.com in November 1997 by Michael Robertson and Greg Flores to allow music to be easily downloaded from the Internet and at the same time start a shake-up in the music industry by breaking unsigned artists on the Web, it was only 14 months until Shawn Fanning, a 19-year-old student at Northeastern University, developed the original Napster application. Three months later, in May 1999 Napster.com was founded to enable sharing of personal music and finding MP3 files online and, with $2mn in seed capital, its first Website was subsequently launched in August 1999. Together MP3 and Napster created a mechanism by which tracks could be uploaded, downloaded, and shared at little or no cost, and certainly one with no IP revenue for the artists and labels.

Now alerted to the issue and facing potential disaster in terms of revenue, the music industry started to get its act together to combat the emerging threat, with an initial copyright infringement suit by the RIAA against Napster on December 8, 1999. Fearing both legal liabilities and problems with bandwidth, Northeastern University, the home of Napster, then quickly led the way for 60 other US universities in blocking student access to the company's Website. This was at about the same time that the US Department of Justice won its first pirating conviction against a 22-year-old Oregon student for illegal distribution of copyrighted material using MP3 technology.

With the Napster suit in progress, on January 21, 2000 the RIAA sued MP3.com, alleging copyright violations by the company's new service giving consumers access to digital copies of their CDs. As their first non-legal reaction to Napster, two weeks later all five major labels then collectively invested in Listen.com, an online music site, to link users to legal MP3 files. Four days later, on February 8, MP3.com hit back filing a suit against the RIAA claiming unfair business practice in its attempt to undermine the company.

On April 13 music artists themselves began to get involved as firstly Metallica sued Napster and three US universities – Southern California, Yale and Indiana – charging them with massive violation of the band's copyrights. This action prompted the three universities to block student access to Napster.com, and rap artist Dr Dre also to sue Napster, and, significantly, thousands of students, thus now putting individuals in the line of fire.

On April 28 the US Federal Court ruled that MP3.com was liable for copyright infringement as claimed by the RIAA, and two weeks later Michael Robertson shut down his Internet site. On June 9 Warner and BMG became the first record companies to settle their own lawsuits against MP3.com that paid the labels between $75mn and $100mn for the right to use their songs on its site. This quickly led to MP3.com allowing individual artists to charge a monthly fee for downloading of their music.

Four days after the Warner/BMG/MP3 settlement, the RIAA followed up with an injunction against Napster in an attempt to shut down the site; and a week later, Napster in turn hired David Boies, the US Government's special counsel in the Microsoft Antitrust Trial, to fight the challenge. On July 26 the RIAA won their injunction, and the following day, Napster appealed for an emergency block to the ruling that threatened to put it out of business.

On August 22 MP3.com reached a settlement with Sony, but two weeks later a federal judge ruled that the company had willfully violated copyrights owned by Universal – a ruling that later forced MP3.com to pay Universal $54mn. The following week, with long-term success for the music industry increasingly likely, independent music groups started to get involved, and Zomba Music also sued MP3. By October 2000 MP3 had come to an agreement with US music publishers giving its users access to over 1 million songs.

Meanwhile, on October 31 Napster, which was by now appealing against an increasing number of lawsuits that were all threatening its future, made a major move as it agreed a strategic alliance with the German media giant Bertelsmann, parent of BMG, stunning some US executives but hence effectively becoming part of the music establishment – albeit a part with many outstanding questions remaining still against it.

Following this, in January 2001 Ebel, an independent German label, agreed an alliance with Napster, and a link was also established between Napster and CD-Now, the online retailer, to use Napster technology to promote music sales. In the same month TVT Records, another independent label, dropped its $1.5bn lawsuit against Napster and, as a major sign of coming into the mainstream, on January 29 Napster itself announced that it would soon start charging subscription fees. In the following month illegal downloads from Napster hit their all-time high of 2.8 billion at the same time as the company promised to deliver $1bn in extra income to the music industry over the next five years by passing on subscription revenue.

In March 2001 Napster finally made significant steps to becoming legal, and blocked 135,000 copyrighted songs from its online service, thus avoiding the threat of the immediate closure originally requested by the RIAA and IFPI. However, the record companies felt that Napster was dragging its feet, and quickly announced fresh legal action on March 28. Moreover, to provide an alternative channel, two days later BMG, EMI and Warner confirmed plans to form MusicNet, an online venture with Real Networks to make their music available over a subscription service. MusicNet effectively became a wholesaler of downloadable music to online retailers, with each track containing new security technologies that limit use and duplication.

This provided the three labels with a fully legal music download capability, the equal of Napster, built with and run by one of the leaders in streaming technology. The following week Sony and Universal agreed a similar relationship to form Duet, later re-christened PressPlay, another music distribution alliance, this time with Yahoo!.

Faced with continued suspicion of Napster, on April 10 BMG abandoned its plan to persuade its rival major labels to join its alliance with the company. The following day, the RIAA considered suing individual executives at Napster as a further escalation and subsequently also to file suits against Aimster, another imitation Internet file-swapping service.

On June 6 Napster signed a deal with MusicNet, allowing it to license the core technology which tracks copyright ownership, although, until Napster could prove that it had finally changed its position and confirmed the ability to operate under copyright laws, its 70 million users would not be able to touch music offered by these three leading labels. It was however unclear what impact the deal would have on the big five record labels' ongoing lawsuit against Napster, which charges it with encouraging widespread piracy through its existing system. Napster was still promising to convert itself into a full subscription business by July 2001.

On May 20, 2001 Universal announced that it was buying MP3.com for $372mn, Michael Robertson joining parent Vivendi's Park Avenue office as special adviser to CEO Jean-Marie Messier.

Status quo

So, within four years of the invention of MP3 technology and with it the ability to potentially disrupt the whole music industry, it appears that the threat from Napster and its imitators – the first round of the battle to protect royalty streams from the Internet – may have been won. Although slow to react, and initially treating the technology more as an opportunity rather than a threat, the music industry got itself aligned and, as the IFPI closed down 15,000 sites containing 300,000 music files in 2000, downloads from Napster fell from the peak of 2.8

billion in February 2001 to 360,000 three months later. How long the current position can be sustained will be a test both of the ingenuity of those who feel that free distribution is paramount, and the ways in which the industry can manage its IP position.

In the meantime, the problems of CD piracy have not gone away. Average piracy rate for CDs is now up to 36%, or nearly 2 billion CDs per annum with the Ukraine, Israel and the Czech Republic the latest hot spots for counterfeit mass production. Lost revenue from royalties now tops $4bn so, even though the Internet threat may have been overcome, as CD prices in retail stores remain arguably far too high and hence continue to propagate the demand for cheap copies, in protecting even its traditional royalty revenue streams, the music industry clearly still has an enormous IP challenge ahead.

KEY INSIGHTS

» The Internet has three dimensions of impact on IP – bypassing, defending and creating.

» Mass sharing of information has supported access to core software through open source.

» Linux is the most prominent example of free access software with no attached IP.

» Defending IP has especially been an issue for software, books and music.

» Software and music piracy via the Internet has spiraled with massive losses of revenue.

» Napster and MP3 cases have brought defending music copyright into the headlines.

» The publishing world has largely embraced the Internet and has not suffered as expected.

» Business methods have been the main area for the creation of new IP using the Internet

» Amazon, Priceline and Google are three prominent examples of new IP.

» Domain name copyright has also become an issue, especially when supporting the brand.

The Global Dimension

What are the impacts of globalization on managing and exploiting IP? Chapter 5 addresses some of the issues and provides insights into some of the implications including:

» the new global frameworks that provide enhanced protection;
» medicines for the developing world;
» bio-colonialism; and
» controlling access to markets.

"Intellectual property rights are foreign to no culture and native to all nations."

Dr Kamil Idris (director general of WIPO)

Faster technology diffusion, market globalization, increased corporate reach, the "global village," and increasingly varied perspectives between the developed and the developing world are all impacting on, and, in many ways, being influenced by the recent growth in scope of intellectual property.

In this chapter we examine the key drivers and consequences of the global dimension for the management of IP. First, the most recent developments in the global framework for gaining and implementing IP protection through the varied relevant bodies are reviewed. These are the key facilitators of global reach and need to be understood. Then we look at some of the consequences of this, and highlight key issues:

» drug availability in the developing world;
» bio-colonialism; and
» controlling access to markets.

Lastly we question whether in some arenas IP protection can be considered to be counter-cultural, and what the implications of this may be.

THE GLOBAL FRAMEWORK

Until recently, global protection for IP was a matter of filing applications in each individual country where you wished to gain protection. Whilst many saw a US patent as the *de facto* standard, in order actively to maintain your IP position globally, protection was formally required. After a slow build-up over the past 30 years, there is now a full framework of legislation in place that will allow intellectual property rights to be enforced throughout the world, giving owners of IP the same rights globally as enjoyed in their home country. The key elements of this framework are:

» WIPO (The World Intellectual Property Organization);
» PCT (The Patent Co-operation Treaty);
» the Madrid and Hague Systems for trademarks and design marks;

» the WTO (World Trade Organization); and, specifically
» TRIPS (The Agreement on Trade Related Aspects of Intellectual Property Rights).

THE WORLD INTELLECTUAL PROPERTY ORGANIZATION

WIPO is responsible for managing the 21 global IP treaties across its 177 member states. Based in Geneva it is an agency of the United Nations with a mandate to administer intellectual property matters recognized by the member states of the UN, including the promotion of IP protection around the world.

WIPO has its roots in two small bureaus set up to administer two of the founding international treaties on intellectual property rights. The first was established around the Paris Convention for the Protection of Industrial Property, which came into force in 1884 to give patents, trademarks and industrial designs the same protection across its 14 member states. The second was the Berne Convention for the Protection of Literary and Artistic Works set up in 1886 to protect and ensure payment for creative works such as novels, songs and drawings. These merged in 1893 and moved first to Berne and then in 1960 to Geneva. Today, WIPO is at the forefront of global IP issues pursuing initiatives such as the Digital Agenda that aims to integrate developing countries into the Internet world through the correct implementation of IP law into their Internet transactions.

THE PATENT CO-OPERATION TREATY

The PCT was established in 1970 to allow inventors to gain protection in a large number of countries by filing a single international patent application. There are currently 108 members of the PCT, and the PCT system is expanding rapidly with the number of applications growing from 2,600 in 1979 to 74,000 in 1999.

With a PCT application an inventor selects those countries in which the patent should be enforced. The PCT application is then sent to one of the appointed receiving offices. This may be the national patent office, the European Patent Office, ARIPO (the African Regional Industrial Property Organization) or EAOP (the Eurasian Patent Office).

Once an application has gained international consent, it cannot be rejected by any of the national offices selected at the time of submission.

It is incidentally often better to make a PCT application and select your domestic country as a designated state rather than file a domestic patent and then extend it via a PCT. Thus, through this approach, organizations can now gain global protection in one go, saving time and money in comparison to making multiple individual applications in separate countries.

THE MADRID AND HAGUE SYSTEMS

Whereas the PCT is specifically focused on patents, the parallel Madrid agreement covers trademarks while the Hague agreement covers industrial designs. These systems are also growing. In 1999 there were 20,000 registrations of marks under the Madrid system equivalent to 250,000 national registrations, and under the Hague system there were 6,750 new or renewed industrial designs.

The present form of the Madrid system dates from 1995 and is administered by the WIPO. Like the PCT, a trademark is applied for at the national bureau, which then presents it to an international bureau, responsible for communicating it to all the national offices in each of the designated states. Assuming they do not reject it within a specified period, normally twelve to eighteen months, it then becomes enforceable for ten years. The Hague system follows the same methodology.

THE WORLD TRADE ORGANIZATION

The WTO has become more involved with IP law as the technical revolution has led to IP becoming a major element of trade, and also to tension between countries. In the 1986–94 Uruguay Round the WTO established the Agreement on Trade Related Aspects of Intellectual Property Rights or "TRIPS". This builds on the conventions administered by WIPO, particularly the Paris and Berne agreements, strengthening some of the areas that were thought to be inadequate; and has also included new areas.

TRIPS

The WTO Agreement on Trade Related Aspects of Intellectual Property Rights, or TRIPS, seeks to bring national practice in IP protection up to a common global standard. The main issues addressed by TRIPS are the basic principles of a trading system for IP; how to give adequate protection; how to enforce IP rights; how to settle disputes; and how it was to be introduced. Most of the countries that have signed up to the WTO after 1995 have agreed to join TRIPS, though this is determined by their individual terms of membership.

The full agreement can be found on the WTO's Website www.wto.org but the highlights are as follows.

» Copyright – TRIPS ensured that computer programs were protected as literary works and so covered by the original Berne Convention.
» Trademarks – service marks were given the same protection as trademarks.
» Geographical indications – the names of some regions or cities have become identifiers of the origin and quality of a type of good, for example "Champagne." As place names these were previously not protected, so TRIPS incorporated provisions to prevent consumers being misled into believing, say, that a cheese is Cheddar just because its manufacturers make this claim. What cannot be protected is the name Cheddar, as it is too generic.
» Patents – these are now to be universally granted for at least twenty years. Governments can refuse to issue a patent for reasons of public order or morality. They can also exclude diagnostic, therapeutic and surgical methods, plants and animals (except micro-organisms) and biological processes for the production of plants or animals (other than microbiological processes). Plant varieties must be protectable by patents or by another approach such as the UPOV (International Union for the Protection of Plant Varieties).
» To prevent a patent holder "sitting" on a valuable patent, governments can also issue "compulsory" licenses allowing a competitor to produce the product or use the process under license, provided this protects the safeguards of the patent holder.

The Uruguay Round took effect on January 1 1995 and, as a consequence, developed countries were given one year to bring their laws into line with the TRIPS agreement. Hence TRIPS is already included in UK, US and most European legislation. Developing countries were, however, given five years to implement the Treaty, and some of the least developed countries have until 2006.

For pharmaceutical and agricultural products, developing countries are therefore now forced to accept the filing of patent applications from the date TRIPS was first implemented, though the actual patent can only be granted when national legislation is in place. This is known as the "mailbox" provision, where applications are stored in a mailbox waiting to be processed. Until then, an inventor is given an exclusive marketing right for five years or until the patent is granted.

SOME IMPLICATIONS OF GLOBAL PROTECTION

While the above descriptions may sound a little dry, the implications are considerable. For companies there is now, for the first time, the opportunity to secure effective and enforceable protection globally. No more black holes for IP protection where, by the manufacture of a product or location of a server in a non-compliant country, pirate products and services can be provided. This is clearly an improvement and something that significantly enhances the grip that owners of IP have on exploitation, and a key tool for more effective management of the IP portfolio. However there is a downside.

Although creating a positive situation for the holders of, for example, pharmaceutical and agricultural patents, the impact on the developing world is far from beneficial.

Medicines for poor people

On April 19 2001, 39 of the world's biggest drug companies announced that they were dropping their lawsuit against the South African government to prevent it importing low-cost copies of their patented drugs to fight HIV and AIDS.

The companies had been seeking to protect their patent rights by forcing the government to buy their proprietary medicines, rather than the "generic" copies that had been made in Brazil and Thailand. As the generic drugs manufacturers did not have to recover the cost of expensive R&D in their prices, they were able to sell the same drugs for a fraction of the normal price.

Though South Africa had implemented TRIPS as a developed nation, thus requiring it to comply with global pharmaceutical patent protection, it had also passed a law in 1997 that allowed it to import generic medicines in the event of a public health crisis. It was this law that the pharmaceutical companies had attempted to rescind. In the eyes of the South African government HIV and AIDS are public health crises and hence they can use generic products.

Oxfam believes that 11 million people, most of them in the least developed countries, die each year from diseases that could be prevented if they had access to affordable medicines. It is agreements such as TRIPS that place effective treatment beyond the reach of the poor. In Kenya, one-quarter of the population is HIV-positive, but only 2% receive anti-retroviral treatment. In Zambia, the cost of treating a single case of childhood pneumonia is half the family's monthly income of US$9. In addition, countries such as India have specifically excluded themselves from being subject to global enforcement of pharmaceutical IP in order that their home generic producers can grow and provide low-cost products for their local markets.

The long-term outcome of the debate is unclear but it appears that TRIPS will not be the all-encompassing panacea that it was intended to be. Although accepted for areas such as copyright and electronics goods, the more contentious pharmaceutical issues may well drive an amendment pretty soon. Clearly managers in the affected industries should be aware of this when making decisions on the reach and value of the IP in their portfolio.

Bio-colonialism

The top 15 crops in the US have annual sales of $50 billion. All come from foreign sources with the bulk of their genetic input coming from developing countries, yet few of these developing countries share in this wealth.

Traditionally, developing countries have derived little benefit from their biodiversity as their genetic resources have been treated as an "unregulated and freely accessible good." In 1992 the global community signed up to the CBD (Convention on Biological Diversity), whose aim was to encourage more innovative approaches, but which also allowed national governments to control access to genetic and biological resources.

With its focus on patenting, TRIPS moves this control to an individual level such as a person or company. Though countries still have some latitude to handle this conflict, if they do not implement a solution they will by default become subject to the UPOV legislation (a part of TRIPS) and so may lose control, the implication being that, through TRIPS, any western corporation can seek and gain protection for a flower, seed or crop that may have been nurtured through careful, iterative husbandry by an indigenous group over the previous millennium.

There is also a second side to the argument. Whereas CBD was seen to be pro-government by following the belief that a government should have control of its biological resources to solve its own problems, UPOV and TRIPS are slanted towards biotechnology with the criteria for UPOV protection favoring the production and use of genetically uniform crops. This may prove to encourage a GM revolution by stealth.

Controlling access to markets

TRIPS gives countries such as the US a head start in patenting areas that other countries are only just beginning to come to terms with. The US is more positive towards granting patents, as the head of the USPTO remarked, "We are in the job of granting patents, not rejecting them." It is worth remembering that although a domestic patent is only enforceable in the home country, no one else in the world can then patent the same invention.

Take business patents, mentioned in Chapter 4 and discussed in more detail in Chapter 6. In 1999, firms filed 2,600 business patents in the US that through PCT will have a global reach. Only 200 were filed in Europe, of which the UK filed 10. To quote Paul Stevens of the law firm Olswang, "American companies are using the existing system and European countries are going to be locked out of markets."

Take for example, the US firm IMS Health. It analyses sales information for the health care industry on behalf of the large drug companies. IMS owns a copyrighted system that divides countries into certain areas called "bricks," and this approach has now become so widespread that its rivals find it difficult to sell their products, as customers want something that follows the IMS approach. Due to IMS' copyright they cannot copy this.

Mario Monti, the European Competition Commissioner, is due to consider the case. Should he rule for IMS then he will be seen to be supporting a monopoly that may be considered to be anti-competitive. If he rules against IMS and forces the company to license its copyright, what incentive will this provide for firms to invest in IP that can create a competitive barrier?

COUNTER-CULTURAL IMPACT

Lastly, there is an underlying issue across many developing countries that from a cultural perspective impedes them from gaining the planned benefits and rewards. TRIPS has largely been developed by the western world that recognizes, above all else, the rights of the individual. However, in some countries, information may be passed down through various ceremonies, teachings or customs and is held communally.

For example, if a drugs company were to develop medicine based on the traditional medicine of an Amazon tribe – who should receive the royalties? Should the patent be allowed as it seeks to change the culture of the community away from the tribe and towards that of the individual? Though TRIPS allows countries to exclude various therapeutic approaches, by doing this it effectively highlights them as being potentially valuable. A drugs company can then develop a process that achieves the same result and patent this.

The opportunities on a global scale are therefore clearly available and, through the recent agreements, can be taken. However within certain arenas, and especially life sciences, the legal frameworks are clearly coming into conflict with ethical and cultural issues. Right now the legislation supports the western multinational rather than the originators of many of the target products. This is a situation that cannot be sustainable in the long term and therefore one which sooner or later will have to change.

KEY INSIGHTS

» Global IP protection has been significantly increased over the last 20 years of the twentieth century.
» The World Intellectual Property Organization has been established to manage treaties across 177 states.
» The Patent Co-operation Treaty allows inventors to gain protection in many countries with a single application.

» The Madrid and Hague Systems have enabled global protection for copyright and design right.
» TRIPS is the WTO agreement that is driving a global standard for IP.
» There is now an effective and enforceable global IP system.
» South Africa has reacted against global pharmaceutical IP by allowing generic drugs for AIDS and HIV.
» Oxfam believes that TRIPS places effective treatment beyond the reach of the poor.
» All of the top 15 US crops come from foreign sources but few of those countries share in the wealth.
» TRIPS allows companies to gain protection for seeds that others have nurtured.
» TRIPS also gives the US a head start in obtaining global patents in areas like business methods that other countries have not yet come to terms with.
» In some countries the idea of IP protecting the individual is counter-cultural.

State of the Art

What is state of the art in managing IP right now? Chapter 6 looks beyond basic capabilities to new issues in highlighting the key emerging themes:

» new types of patents;
» new types of companies; and
» new strategies.

In such a rapidly evolving arena, state of the art in managing intellectual property is developing and gaining interest across industries. For many organizations for whom managing IP is a new issue, state of the art should be seen in the perspective of best practice, and the putting in place of the internal capability to define an IP strategy, implement it, and thus create value. Many of the elements that are associated with this are detailed elsewhere, and particularly in Chapters 2 and 10.

By contrast, for companies who are experienced in managing IP at a basic level, state of the art is more to do with what are the emerging practices that are defining the leading edge. For those seeking to evolve rather than establish their IP management capability, the implications of the new types of patents that are being granted, the approaches of the new types of development companies that are exploiting IP, and the new strategies that are being adopted by leading players to create value are the topics that are of interest, and the ones that we address here.

NEW TYPES OF PATENTS

Algorithms and business methods

No area has generated more heated debate in the IP arena than the patenting of business processes and software in which the US leads the charge. Consider recent statistics from the European Patent Office (EPO), where US nationals filed 52% of all patents for business methods though they filed only 28% of patents overall. Similarly at the United Kingdom Patent Office, where 31% of all business method patents were filed by US nationals, compared with 10% of patents overall. How and why have business methods come to be patentable and what exactly is a business method?

In 1952 a modification to the 1836 Patent Act established criteria for the patentability of inventions in the US; namely that they belong to a domain of statutory subject matter, are new, useful, and not obvious to a person skilled in the art at the time of the invention. Individuals and companies were allowed to patent processes, methods, machines and composition of matter, but not the "basic tools of science" as this was seen as a hindrance to rather than a promotion of progress. There were also specific exceptions for concepts that were considered to be too abstract, such as ideas, laws of nature or natural phenomena. Also included were mathematical algorithms and business methods.

The landmark case that overturned the latter two exceptions was State Street Bank vs. Signature Financial in 1998. The bank had wished to license a financial software program from Signature, who refused and were subsequently taken to court on the basis that the software could not be patented as an algorithm or business method and so in reality the bank had no need to request a license.

The patenting of algorithms had been refined by three cases commonly referred to by the shorthand "Freeman-Walter-Abele." These established that patents for algorithms could be considered to be patents for a process (and hence patentable) if they related to the application of the algorithm and were not related to the abstract idea of the algorithm itself.

At the lowest level, the Federal District Court applied this test and found that there was no patent that Signature could claim for its software. This was upheld at the District Court, but then rejected at the higher Federal Circuit. It ruled that any transformation of data resulting in a "useful concrete and tangible result" should be patentable. As the result of the algorithm applied by the software was a share price that was relied on by the IRS, it was deemed that this was a practical application of an algorithm and so patentable.

Financial and Internet companies have been quick to exploit this change in the USPTO's perception and now they are looking to patent under the title of business methods: gauging consumer habits, marketing, inducing customers to buy, charging for goods or services, accounting, creating new markets and trading, distributing products or services, and generalizing methods of production and manufacturing (e.g. "just-in-time" production).

As detailed in Chapter 4, examples of well-known patents include Priceline's claim to a computer-based buyer-driven reverse auction procedure, which they are using to sue Microsoft Expedia for selling airline tickets by the same method, and Amazon's 1-click shopping method which they have used to sue Barnes & Noble (where the 1-click is now a 2-click).

In Europe the EPO still insists that patents must relate to a technical field and be concerned with a technical problem so the legislation explicitly excludes business methods. A computer program running on a computer is not patentable, but where the result of the program is a contribution to a field that is patentable, the program would be allowed. For example, Vicom was awarded a patent for a mathematical method to enhance the quality of a digital image, as the image-processing field is patentable whereas programs for data processing cannot be patented as the field of programming is excluded.

However, it is anticipated that wording agreed at the Uruguay Round of the GATT Accord will supersede certain elements of the European Patent Convention, so bringing Europe into line with the US and making the patenting of software far easier. Today, even the global consultancies such as KPMG are beginning to explore ways of patenting their consultancy processes.

And the future? See US Patent 6004596 – it gives JM Smucker a patent over its version of a peanut butter and jelly sandwich!

NEW TYPES OF COMPANIES

Development companies

The traditional business model has been that a company develops a product or service that may incorporate new technologies or innovative steps, then engineers this for production, produces it and manages its sales and marketing. The money generated from the first product funds the R&D for a second product and so on.

The use of patents has allowed this value chain to become broken, and development and commercialization to become separate things, done by separate companies, with the patent acting as the formal transfer mechanism between the two. Traditionally this has been the preserve of the academic institutions, but now a new breed of company has been able to generate considerable revenues through licensing and sales of the IP that they have developed but which someone else markets.

Examples of these development companies include the Generics Group, Accentus, and Scipher of the UK, whereas an example of a commercialization company is BTG, the British Technology Group. Listed in 1995, it has achieved notable successes in commercializing BeneFix, a drug for hemophiliacs to help blood clotting, and MLC memory for expanding the capacity of flash memory. Ian Harvey, the chief executive of BTG points to this being a UK phenomenon and claims that "There aren't many look-alikes in the US." This perspective is based on the fact that, due to their size, US corporations such as IBM and Xerox have the capacity to have their own internal groups dedicated to IP exploitation. In the UK, corporate size and focus has helped such independent commercialization companies to grow or be spun out of their parent organizations.

Patent exchanges

As companies realize that they have non-core patents which they would like to license or sell, the challenge becomes how to reach out to a large enough audience? One way is to use a new breed of Website that classifies and describes the patents, taking a commission on those sold through the site. One example is www.yet2.com, which is supported by a host of large companies such as Pitney Bowes, Motorola, and Siemens.

Another more specialized example is the Virtual Component Exchange at www.vcx.org that offers to license IP cores for semiconductor chips. Manufacturers would license a number of cores and build them into an integrated circuit. Examples of companies offering their IP include ARM with their non-leading RISC processor cores, Arc Cores and Imagination Technology Group. The VCX site also helps companies negotiate licenses through their TransactionWare software.

At the other end of the spectrum are sites such as the Walmart Innovation Center that invites anyone to send in details of their invention. The Center then assesses whether any part of it can be patented and offers to help in this in return for a commission.

NEW STRATEGIES

Using patents as an aggressive tool

Perhaps one of the biggest changes today has been seeing intellectual property as a new type of legal protective mechanism instead of a revenue opportunity or defensive tool. The greatest demonstration of this can be seen in the new tactics in which companies are using patents to attack a competitor. Here are some of these tactics.

» *Patent walls or patent thickets* to protect an area so that competitors will come nowhere near it. An example is Gillette and its Sensor shaver. Though there were seven designs that could have been used, the company selected the one that could be protected with the most patents. The razor has over 20 patents covering its functionality right through to the click of the box when opening it.

» *Land grabbing* or using patents to claim a hold in a new market. However, before entering a new field you must analyze all the existing patents in order to understand the available niche. One technique for doing this is by analyzing patent databases such as Delphion to see what topics have been patented in the field, and also to see the direction in which different companies are moving. In simplistic terms, if you were looking to enter the printer field, an analysis of the topic "printer" could reveal that a competitor had filed multiple ink-jet patterns between 1993 and 1997, but from 1997 onwards began filing those related to laser printers. This shows its movement away from ink-jet and into laser.

» *Cross licensing* – finding where a potential customer infringes your patents, suing them and then offering to settle by a cross license in which they agree to buy certain volumes of your products. An expert at this is IBM (see Chapter 7).

» *Restricting* involves building patents around a competitor's initial patent or product. For example, patenting the production process a competitor must use to manufacture their product would prevent them from ever making it.

Patent pooling

Patent pooling is where a company assigns its patented technology to a "pool" of patents that must all be licensed if a company is to build a certain product. It is a way of creating a *de facto* standard.

Licensees prefer to license from the pool, which acts as a one-stop shop, rather than have to negotiate directly with each company. It also helps them by quickly identifying all the patents they need to license. None of the companies contributing into the pool can withhold the licensing of their patents to a company unless the pool acts in an unreasonable manner and they rely on the pool to enforce the patents.

One example is the MPEG-2 Video and Systems standard. MPEG is a video compression standard and forms the basis for storing, transmitting and displaying digital video. Its pool is managed by MPEG LA, a US company, and has more than 275 patents. Licensees such as Hitachi, Pioneer and Motorola have already taken out licenses.

Another example involves DVDs, where there are two competing pools called 6C and 3C who are demanding royalties of between 3.5% and 4% per player. Both share IP and development; in the case of 6C between Toshiba, Matsushita, JVC, Mitsubishi, Hitachi, and Time Warner; and with 3C between Phillips, Sony, and Pioneer. The DVD Forum is trying to bring both pools together to form one global standard.

Finally Bluetooth, the technology underpinning new wireless applications (see Chapter 7), was initiated by Ericsson in 1994, but the IP exists as a pool owned by a special interest group led by Ericsson, IBM, Nokia, and Toshiba. This enables both shared development and wider and faster market penetration.

Financial strategies

Some IP has such strong and reliable income streams that companies can securitize them to receive the income today instead of in the future. Called Asset Backed Securitization or ABS, it is a growing phenomenon, particularly in the music industry.

The first to offer these types of bond was the singer David Bowie when Prudential Securities issued $55mn worth of fifteen-year bonds backed by the royalties from the publishing and recording rights to 300 of his songs. Other singers said to be considering ABS include Crosby, Stills & Nash, The Rolling Stones, Prince, Neil Diamond, and Luciano Pavarotti. The concept is just as applicable to any entertainer including popular, classical or operatic entertainers; or conductors, successful authors, movie producers or TV entertainers.

Another advantage, particularly with start-ups, is that a lot of patents or even patent applications give the company the appearance of being asset-rich, and so more substantial than may actually be the case. Once the patents are granted it is sometimes possible to insure the patents from an infringement action against them, thus guaranteeing a risk-free royalty stream that may be financed in some form.

KEY INSIGHTS

» For many organizations, state of the art in managing IP is the establishment of an IP management capability.

» For organizations seeking to evolve their capability, state of the art means new types of patents, new types of companies and new strategies.

» Patenting of business methods encourages companies to exploit the opportunities available.

» Commercialization of IP developed elsewhere has become a distinct focus for some new companies.

» Patent exchanges are allowing licensing and selling opportunities for non-core IP to become a dynamic marketplace.

» Some organizations are now using patents as an aggressive tool to lock out competitors.

» Patent pooling is helping to create *de facto* standards for new technologies.

» IP with strong and reliable revenue streams is now being used for securitization.

In Practice

How are leading companies exploiting IP? Chapter 7 answers this by using six different examples of the approaches being adopted by some of the leaders.

- » How IBM generated over $1bn of revenue from its patent database using cross licensing.
- » How Jerome Lemelson and the Lemelson Foundation have generated IP revenue.
- » How Kodak failed to break Polaroid's patent wall.
- » How the merchandising rights of the Teletubbies have been exploited.
- » How Qualcomm has used its patents to underpin the 3G wireless world.
- » How Ericsson has driven the spread of Bluetooth technology through shared IP.
- » Why Texas Instruments paid $400mn for a company with sales of $13mn.

There are many different examples of how companies have managed intellectual property. Several of these, including Amazon, the music industry, Linux, BTG, and the pharmaceutical companies are highlighted elsewhere in this book. In this chapter, we have selected a number of key examples that we have chosen to go into in more depth. Each of these illustrates a different element of managing IP, but all provide insights of how to generate value from IP.

» *Cross licensing IP*: how IBM generated over $1bn of revenue from its patent database using cross licensing.
» *Revenue from IP*: how Jerome Lemelson and the Lemelson Foundation have generated IP revenue.
» *Patent walls*: how Kodak failed to break Polaroid's patent wall.
» *Merchandising*: how the merchandising rights of the Teletubbies have been exploited.
» *Creating a standard*: how Qualcomm has used its patents to underpin the 3G wireless world.
» *Sharing IP*: how Ericsson has driven the spread of Bluetooth technology through shared IP.
» *The value of patents*: why Texas Instruments paid $400mn for a company with sales of $13mn.

IBM: MINING PATENTS FOR GOLD

In late 1998 Lou Gerstner, head of IBM, was concerned at the low return on the company's $5bn R&D budget. He challenged three of his executives to find a way to generate a greater return from the money the company was investing.

The solution proposed by the three was for IBM to become a component supplier and integrator for a range of OEM customers. The board agreed their strategy, grandly titled "IBM's OEM strategy for the twenty-first century" in late August 1998, and soon the IBM Technology Group or ITG was born. This new division combined the mass storage division, which previously had been IBM's component supply operation, microelectronics, printing and network hardware division.

The subtle strategy of the group was to use IBM's massive array of patents to challenge hardware manufacturers for potential infringements, and encourage them to settle through cross licensing agreements. Some of these would be in the form of IBM supplying the company with its components in lieu of royalties.

This database currently holds over 12,000 patents, with another 2,500 being added each year. For eight years in the 1990s IBM filed more patents at the USPTO than any other company. Its current patent portfolio covers the fundamentals of computing, cryptography, software, storage networking, PC and server architectures, and semi-conductor design and manufacturing. It is said that anyone working in the computer industry has at some time infringed an IBM patent!

The greatest change in IBM's thinking was that instead of using its patents as a defensive mechanism to protect its research work, it began to use them as an aggressive commercial weapon to generate sales. In the words of Tony Baker, head of Business Development at ITG, "Getting a return on that intellectual property is a very active program at IBM." In some instances ITG understood what technology they wanted from their competitors and used a potential patent infringement case to get it. The list of new licensees includes the cream of the computing world!

» The storage company EMC agreed to purchase $3bn in IBM disk drives in a cross licensing deal to resolve a potential dispute when their previous licensing agreement with IBM expired in 1998.

» Cisco signed a cross licensing deal which led to a $2bn transaction in 1999 whereby IBM exited the network hardware market by selling its routing and switching patents to Cisco, in return for Cisco agreeing to purchase IBM storage devices and PCs.

» Acer required access to IBM's patents for the next generation of its PCs and computing devices. In a deal valued at $8bn, Acer will buy LCDs, storage devices, networking and processors from IBM, whilst IBM will purchase $1bn of Acer LCDs which it will resell.

» 3Com was eager to access IBM's patent portfolio to speed up development, and so signed a $2bn cross licensing deal in which each will get access to the other's patents.

» Dell agreed a $16bn component deal to supersede a previous licensing agreement. This effectively saved Dell tens of millions of dollars as, rather than having to pay IBM license fees and buy its components, the company agreed to buy components from IBM in lieu of licensing fees. This was expenditure it would have had to incur anyway.

In a later case, IBM wished to use Dell's ordering system, its greatest competitive advantage and something Dell had protected with two business model patents. In a second deal, initiated by IBM, Dell cross licensed these patents in return for formalizing a licensing agreement on another set of patents it had been found to be infringing. In IBM's words "This removed an inhibitor to a potential relationship."

The success of ITG has been phenomenal. In the first six months of 1999 it generated roughly $8bn in revenues in a mix of pure licensing revenues and component sales with a goal of close to $20bn by the end of 2002.

JEROME LEMELSON

It is unusual to highlight an individual, but Jerome Lemelson was no ordinary individual. He was granted more than 500 patents, four short of Thomas Edison, some of which date back to the 1950s. Until his death in 1997, he spent a lot of his time suing major companies for infringement of his patents that covered essential parts of dozens of products in common use today, including the VCR, camcorder, Walkman, cordless phone, fax machine, data and word processing systems, and industrial robots.

His inventing really began in 1954 when he applied for his first automation patents, including his "machine vision" system: a combination of computers, robotics, and electro-optics that allowed assembly-line robots to perform multiple operations on an item, including quality checking.

In the 1960s, he won licensing offers for his industrial ideas, including an automated warehouse system. In 1974, he licensed to Sony the audiocassette drive mechanism that made possible the Walkman. In 1977, ironically, his first patent application for the camcorder was rejected, as the examiner considered portable video recorders were an impossibility! In 1981, IBM bought about 20 Lemelson patents for data and word processing systems.

In the mid-90s he counter-sued Motorola and a number of car manufacturers over 17 of his patents in the areas of machine vision, bar codes and other processes. Motorola agreed to settle by paying an undisclosed sum to his philanthropic foundation. This, along with all the proceeds from the hundreds of actions brought by his foundation, is used to fund educational programs at MIT and a number of other US universities.

Suits by the Lemelson Foundation are now so common that there is a dedicated Website (www.lemelsonpatents.com) and attorneys that specialize in defending "Lemelson suits" against *Fortune 500* companies!

KODAK VS. POLAROID: AN INSURMOUNTABLE WALL

In the late 1960s the instant photography market began to boom, with sales of cameras accounting for 15% of the market. One company, Polaroid, whose annual sales were 10% of that of its arch-rival Kodak Eastman, dominated it.

Whilst developing its technology, Polaroid had been careful to protect it with a wall of patents preventing its competitors from copying it. However, the market was so attractive that in 1969 Kodak's R&D division decided to begin "Project 130" to develop its own instant camera and film.

In its path were two obstacles: first the patents, and second, Kodak had worked with Polaroid in a joint development project during which Polaroid had revealed some of its future products to Kodak's engineers under a non-disclosure agreement. Mindful of any potential infringement, Kodak had even taken the step of hiring an attorney to advise them during their R&D.

As Polaroid was already selling a product, customers had come to recognize its camera as the instant camera in much the same way that early Hoovers became synonymous with the vacuum cleaner. If Kodak was to compete it would have to develop something similar, but the patents and confidentiality agreement prevented this.

Faced with a potential deadlock, Kodak pursued a strategy of allowing its staff to develop designs that might infringe the patents, and even issued a memorandum to its staff saying that they "should not be constrained by what an individual feels is potential patent infringement." At the same time, Kodak worked to rule that any potential infringement would be invalid as the patents were not strong enough to be upheld legally.

On April 20, 1976 Kodak finally launched its new instant camera to much fanfare. Seven days later Polaroid responded with a lawsuit claiming infringement of 12 of its patents. The ensuing trial took nine years and decided that Kodak had infringed seven patents. It was then a further five years before the scale of the damages could be determined. By the time it finished in 1990, having peaked in 1978, 35mm compacts, and the advent of digital photography had largely superseded the instant camera market.

What was the total cost? The best estimate is a total of $3bn. Of this, $925mn was in damages, $1.5bn was the money lost in the closure of Kodak's instant camera manufacturing plant, 700 workers had to be laid off, $500mn was spent buying back all the 16 million cameras that had already been sold, legal fees amounted to $100mn and the remainder was the written-off cost of R&D.

In addition to the trial, Kodak then faced a class action lawsuit from people who had bought their cameras. To settle this it established a $150mn fund to compensate the owners with payments of between $50 and $70 each. Polaroid's patent wall thus destroyed Kodak's instant camera business.

TELETUBBIES: CHILD'S PLAY?

The Teletubbies are Tinky Winky, Dipsy, La La and Po, large baby-like characters each in a different, bright color, speaking in a simple language such as "Eh-oh." They were created by Ragdoll Productions in response to a request by the BBC for a program aimed at two-year-olds – a slot it believed was not being addressed by its current range of children's productions. Since their first screening on the BBC in 1997, it is estimated that over a billion children in 120 countries around the world had seen them by 2001.

Most of the income from a program such as *Teletubbies* does not come from the sales to the TV stations but from the merchandising rights. These are licensed to third parties allowing them to produce items such as videos, T-shirts, souvenirs and other items, with a likeness of the original characters. Copyright and a trademark on the name protect the likeness. Given the huge profits that can be generated from a successful series, these rights are extremely valuable and one of the key things in managing them is protecting them.

The creators, Ragdoll Productions, licensed the rights to BBC World-wide for the corporation to sub-license to merchandisers in specific territories. In the US, the rights holder was itsy bitsy Entertainment. For receiving a share of the income, both organizations are responsible for policing and co-prosecuting any potential infringements.

BBC Worldwide has been active in defending the rights to protect its value; it has requested the removal of images of the Teletubbies from numerous Websites; in March 1999 the BBC sued Wal-Mart for selling dolls called Bubbly Chuppies which in the BBC's view were too similar, and it also considered taking action against an individual who had registered the domain names teletubbies.com and teletubbies.co.uk.

The success of the management of the Teletubbies IP can be shown by Kenn Viselman, the CEO of itsy bitsy Entertainment who, when the Teletubbies were introduced into the US on the PBS channel, stated that: "You're looking at a major multimillion-dollar property." He was right – in October 2000, it was reported that since 1997 the Teletubbies had generated over £1bn in merchandising of which the BBC alone has received £90mn.

Today the Teletubbies are licensed in 90 countries and translated into 35 languages, the most recent being Russian where they are shown on state television under the name "TelePuzikis."

QUALCOMM: GAINING PREDOMINANCE IN 3G MOBILE THROUGH IP EXPLOITATION

Qualcomm is one of the world's fastest growing companies and regu-larly tops ratings for strategic and operational excellence. The company has shipped over 200 million chipsets and provides software to enable advanced communication, particularly through mobile devices. Like ARM in the UK, Qualcomm saw its future in revenue generated from licensing leading-edge technology and, over the past few years, has positioned itself accordingly.

Qualcomm started life in San Diego in 1985 as a provider of contract R&D services to the Californian aerospace and defense industries. Over the next ten years the company became the largest fabless semiconductor producer in the world but chose to focus on commercializing its wireless CDMA expertise that now generates substantial revenues from licensing. Qualcomm now has over 1000 engineers dedicated to CDMA technology development and over 1300 patents granted or pending in the US alone.

The CDMA (Code Division Multiple Access) technology, introduced commercially into the market by Qualcomm in 1995, was originally developed by the US government. CDMA codes separate transmissions so multiple data streams can share the same radio channel. It enables very high-speed transmission of up to 2 megabits per second compared to 9.6 kilobits with current GSM technology. CDMA2000, the latest digital version of the CDMA technology, is specifically designed for 3G mobile communications and its growth is accelerating rapidly as licenses are issued and CDMA-based 3G mobile products are launched.

Qualcomm's main competitors in the mobile technology arena are Ericsson and Nokia, whose 2G GSM technology has dominated the European and many Asian markets. Within the US, three different and non-interoperable technologies, one of which was Qualcomm's IS-95, competed for 2G mobile, but none has ever achieved dominance. However, in a bid to create a global standard for 3G mobile, in 1999 Ericsson and Qualcomm signed an agreement to make CDMA2000 the world standard with both companies supporting the technology through patent cross licenses. Nokia and Qualcomm were discussing a similar agreement in July 2001.

In 1999, Qualcomm spun-off its consumer products division to Kyocera and increased gross margin from 32% to 62%. In July 2000, the company announced that it was spinning-off its integrated circuit and system software businesses so that it could concentrate more on the CDMA2000 technology and its future evolution. Although this was scrapped a year later due to the downturn in the technology sector, it highlighted Qualcomm's aim to have its main revenue streams as licenses from its patents for CDMA and other wireless technologies rather than from manufacturing.

Qualcomm is actively licensing its CDMA technology especially in the US, to the likes of Microsoft and Motorola; in Japan, to Matsushita and Mitsubishi; and in Korea to LG Telecom and Intercube. By 2001, over 100 communications equipment manufacturers had taken out licenses. All licensees pay the same flat rate royalty per chipset, thus guaranteeing Qualcomm a predictable and steady revenue growth. Revenue for 2000 was over $3bn, leading some analysts to predict that, due to its pre-eminent position in CDMA technology, Qualcomm will dominate this industry by 2005.

BLUETOOTH: SHARING IP TO MAXIMIZE TECHNOLOGY APPLICATION

With the experience of jointly defining the GSM standard for mobile communications with Nokia, for Ericsson, the Swedish telecommunications company, when deciding how best to exploit its Bluetooth wireless technology, partnership was a clear favorite. Essentially a low cost, low power, short range, yet fast and reliable radio interface that can act, for example, between mobile phones, their accessories and other data products, Bluetooth was first envisaged in 1994. Ericsson realized that, as it had nearly done with GSM, the secret to ensuring take-up of the technology would be to establish quickly a truly global standard, and to do this with other lead companies.

In 1997, the company therefore approached several other manufacturers of portable electronic devices to develop the wireless technology. The following year Ericsson, IBM, Intel, Nokia, and Toshiba duly formed the Bluetooth Special Interest Group leading on to the release of version 1.0 of the technology in 1998. This technology comprises both hardware and software. The principle adopted by Ericsson is that by creating a core group who have stakes in the underlying IP, they can share development effort both in terms of cost and resource and, at the same time, address a far wider market than could have been achieved individually.

With high levels of interest fuelled by the rapidly converging mobile and computing sectors, Bluetooth has quickly gained a leading foothold. Although there are competitors such as 802.11b-based Wi-Fi high-speed wireless LAN, 3Com, Lucent Technologies, Microsoft and Motorola all joined in as promoters of Bluetooth in 2000, as the first products using the technology began to appear on the market. From Motorola's perspective, it was essential that they became part of the group as the combined product set across all companies will, as far as the company is concerned, set the standard. In addition, only by being at the heart of the development activities could they too share learning and experience as part of "an organization whose whole is greater than the sum of its parts."

With this partnership firmly in place to drive and promote development, Ericsson then created Ericsson Technology Licensing specifically to license the Bluetooth technology and help companies such as South Korea's Samsung build Bluetooth technology into their PDA, printer and network products. One year later, membership of the Bluetooth adopter Special Interest Group had passed 2000 – virtually every major communications and electronics company in the world – and Bluetooth is the fastest ever growing *de facto* standard. Forecasts by Cahners-Instat anticipate that by 2005 700 million Bluetooth devices will be shipped annually – all using the same core technology underpinned by the shared IP.

AMATI COMMUNICATIONS: VALUING THE FUTURE

What is the value of leading edge patents? Ask John Cioffi, the CEO of Amati Communications. His company was a spin-out of Stanford University and one of the leading developers of Digital Subscriber Line (xDSL) technology. This new generation of xDSL modems allowed data to be sent over telephone lines more than 100 times faster than a standard 56K analogue modem.

The company had already licensed its technology to companies such as Alcatel, Analog Devices, and Motorola, but despite this had lost $30mn over the past 12 months and only achieved revenues of $13mn. It was also under threat from AT&T that was trying to prevent Amati's version of xDSL being chosen as the future standard in preference to their own.

Who then would want to acquire such a company? Answer, Texas Instruments, who agreed to acquire the company for $395mn. Why? For the 25 patents the company owned, which they believed would catapult them to the forefront of xDSL technology.

TI developed Digital Signal Processors or DSPs. These chips executed instruction sets at ultra fast speeds and TI was looking to get them incorporated into xDSL modems in order to exploit a market expected to be worth $6bn. TI and Amati had already been working together to develop a new xDSL/DSP chip that once in a modem could also be updated using software downloads. Buying Amati protected this position.

In the words of Rich Templeton, president of TI's semiconductor group: "The combination of Amati's DSL technology and TI's digital signal processing solutions will enable faster, more reliable access to the Internet and the ability to use a single existing phone line to simultaneously access voice, data and video."

Following the sale John Cioffi returned to his job as an engineering professor, having started Amati during a sabbatical in 1991. And AT&T? Following Amati being chosen as the future standard, they became a customer!

Key Concepts and Thinkers

Who are the key people and what have they contributed to the world of managing intellectual property? This chapter identifies the major contributors in three core areas:

» managing intellectual property;
» intellectual capital; and
» new perspectives.

Managing IP is clearly a wide and varied subject. It covers multiple aspects from understanding the latest development, defining an appropriate strategy and ensuring that there is organizational alignment and support. Within this arena there are notably a few researchers, commentators and service providers who have highlighted varied issues.

From the growing number of publications that are addressing aspects of managing intellectual property, we have selected nine key people whose thoughts and ideas provide a range of opinions and thoughts about the subject:

» Paul Goldstein on international IP;
» Kevin Rivette on the hidden value in IP;
» James Boyle on emergent IP issues;
» Jessica Litman on IP and the Internet;
» Thomas Stewart on intellectual capital;
» Patrick Sullivan on profiting from intellectual capital;
» John Howkins on copyright in the media industries;
» Lester Thurow on the future of the IP system; and
» Seth Shulman on the ownership of knowledge.

PAUL GOLDSTEIN: INTERNATIONAL IP

Paul Goldstein is professor of law at Stanford specializing in intellectual property and international copyright. He is widely recognized as a leading authority on IP, especially copyright, and is frequently called upon as an expert at international government meetings. He has authored five books including *Copyright's Highway: from Gutenberg to the Celestial JukeBox.*

His most recent works are *International Copyright: Principles, Law and Practice,* and *International Intellectual Property Law: Cases and Materials.* Together, these two volumes provide the authoritative guide to IP today. They are references for many scholars and practitioners of IP and include:

» a complete analysis of national laws across the IP arena;
» choice of law;
» international treaties;

» trade agreements including TRIPS and European directives; and
» IP applications in practice.

These are the definitive texts for managing IP today and are commonly seen as being indispensable.

KEVIN RIVETTE: REMBRANDTS IN THE ATTIC

A former patent attorney, Kevin Rivette is now chairman of Aurigin Systems (see Chapter 9), an organization that develops IP management software for clients. He is one of the leading consultants on how companies are facing the challenges of gaining more value from their IP portfolios. In perhaps the most recognized book on IP management in recent years, Kevin and his co-author David Kline explore some of the major issues facing organizations today.

Offering practical advice for competing in today's IP arena, the key issues addressed include:

» the emerging IP battlefield – what and where;
» creating an inventory – discover what IP you have;
» IP strategy – mapping business development;
» IP focus – putting IP at the heart of the organization;
» patent mining – how to find the hidden treasures;
» offensive use of IP – creating patent walls;
» seeing where your competitors are heading; and
» new areas of protection – IP and the Internet.

Using examples including IBM, Microsoft, Xerox, Gillette, Lucent, and Priceline.com to support the cases made, this is a good management text for providing a coherent and engaging understanding of the IP world.

Link

www.rembrandtsintheattic.com

JAMES BOYLE: SOFTWARE AND SPLEENS

James Boyle is professor of law at Duke Law School and writes on legal and social theory on issues from political correctness to authorship in law and literature. His *New York Times* article "Sold-Out" argued that intellectual property is one of the most significant forms of wealth and power in an information society and that IP rights are being expanded too far and too fast.

His award-winning book *Sharmans, Software and Spleens: Law and the Construction of the Information Society* examined the emergent issues of ownership of genetic information, artificial intelligence, the power of information ownership, the right to privacy, and the right of publicity. In it he covers a wide range of IP applications including patenting of spleens, consumer databases, direct advertising, and ethnobotany. He argues that contemporary concepts of intellectual property are based on outmoded ideas of selfhood that is counter-productive in an information society.

JESSICA LITMAN: IP ON THE INTERNET

Jessica Litman is professor of law, Wayne State University, Detroit, where she teaches courses in copyright law, Internet law and trademarks and unfair competition. Professor Litman is the author of many articles on copyright. Her work has been cited by the Supreme Court and reprinted in House hearings. She is a member of the American Intellectual Property Association, the Association for Teaching and Research in Intellectual Property, and serves on the advisory board of Cyberspace Law Abstracts, and the ACLU Committee on Intellectual Property and the Internet.

In *Protecting Intellectual Property on the Internet*, Jessica Litman shows how the World Wide Web has the potential to restructure copyright laws. It deals with several complex issues relating to the balance between control and access:

» regulation in a free access medium;
» collapse of territoriality in a global marketplace;
» charging royalties to users of the Internet; and
» relevance of current legislation.

Underpinned with a history of the development of copyright law in the US and how we can work within an emerging new control regime, this is a useful insight into a complex and technical area.

THOMAS A. STEWART: INTELLECTUAL CAPITAL

Thomas A. Stewart is a member of the board of directors of *Fortune* magazine where he has a monthly column "The Leading Edge." He pioneered the concept of intellectual capital in a series of articles that earned him an international reputation as the leading expert on the subject.

His book, *Intellectual Capital: The New Wealth of Organizations* (1997) is considered a groundbreaking publication. Using the argument that knowledge is now the most important element in economics and the chief driver of how and why we work, it provides both vision and practical application. The key issues covered include:

» the emergence of the information age;
» the links between information, knowledge and intellectual capital;
» leveraging intellectual capital for competitive advantage;
» structural capital – the knowledge retained within the organization;
» human capital – the knowledge held by the employees;
» the value of IP such as brands, copyright and patents as tangible intellectual capital; and
» managing the assets both hard and soft for improved performance.

Examples are drawn from across industries. As the key text on intellectual capital and the inherent links with intellectual property, this book is an excellent and accessible background read.

Link

www.fortune.com

PATRICK SULLIVAN: PROFITING FROM INTELLECTUAL CAPITAL

Patrick Sullivan is the author of a number of books on managing IP including *Technology Licensing: Corporate Strategies for Maximizing Value and Value Driven Intellectual Capital*, and *How to Convert Intangible Corporate Assets in Market Value*, which provides an executive handbook to intangible assets and their value.

Profiting from Intellectual Capital brings together a collection of key ideas for managing intellectual assets, including a number of best practices of companies at the leading edge of IP management. Split into three sections, the book addresses:

» concepts of intellectual capital, assets and property;
» managing, measuring, and monitoring intellectual capital; and
» techniques for extracting value from intellectual capital using IP.

Using examples including Dow Chemical, IBM, Xerox, Rockwell International, Hewlett-Packard, and Skandia, this book is a comprehensive and coherent overview.

JOHN HOWKINS: MAKING MONEY FROM COPYRIGHT

With a background in media, John Howkins has advised many TV, film and other content delivery companies on their strategies for exploiting the value in their IP.

His first book, *The Creative Economy: How People Make Money from Ideas*, proposes that creativity and the exploitation of the associated copyright will be the dominant economic form of the twenty-first century. Not restricted to just copyright but also covering a number of other IP forms and issues, this book addresses:

» the value of IP in the creative economy;
» creativity and the creation of IP;
» impacts of recent globalization on IP;
» the emergence of patent offices as the banks for IP;
» IP in the creative industries, from advertising and architecture to TV and video;
» managing creativity; and
» IP in the new economy.

Examples are taken mainly from the film and music industries. Although not a global picture of how to manage and exploit IP, this is a useful insight into IP in the media world.

Link

www.penguin.com

LESTER THUROW: CHALLENGING THE *STATUS QUO*

Dr Lester Thurow is professor of management and economics at MIT and focuses on international economics, public finance, macroeconomics and income distribution economics. He writes for a number of US and international newspapers and appears regularly as a commentator on TV. A prolific author, particularly in the arena of global economics, in 1977 he wrote a major piece on intellectual property for the Harvard Business Review. *Needed: a New System of Intellectual Property* argued the case for a major overhaul of the IP system.

Given the fundamental shifts in technology and the economic landscape, Thurow argues that the current system of intellectual property rights is unworkable and ineffective. A system that was set up to patent mechanical devices such as gearboxes cannot cope with the more complex challenges of today such as the invention of a new gene. He also points out that, contrary to the desires and intent of recent global frameworks for IP such as TRIPS, every developing country knows that those such as Taiwan, Indonesia, Mexico and Turkey that have caught up with the West, have done so by copying. Thus the new systems are unsustainable.

Thurow proposes a new system that balances production and distribution of new ideas, where laws are enforceable, disputes should be resolved quickly, and the differences between public and private knowledge, the needs of developed and developing countries, and the variety of requirements from differing industries are all in turn accommodated.

SETH SHULMAN: *OWNING THE FUTURE*

Seth Shulman is a freelance writer and author. A regular contributor to MIT's *Technology Review*, he has particular knowledge in the field of technology development and exploitation. His recent book *Owning the Future* questions whether patented ideas will ultimately help or hinder innovation.

Questioning the concept that freedom of information is growing, this engaging book addresses:

» trends in the ownership of knowledge;
» corporations' use of IP tools to control knowledge;

» the implications of this control on the freedom of exchange of ideas;
» the long-term economic impact of knowledge control; and
» examples of knowledge monopolies.

Using examples from across the high technology world, from pharmaceuticals and genetic engineering to computers, this is a wake-up call to the impact that knowledge monopolies are having on the world.

Link

www.technologyreview.com

Resources

So where can you go for help? Who are useful sources of knowledge and insight? Chapter 9 identifies organizations and publications in three areas:

» patent offices and IP associations;
» advisory organizations; and
» international publications.

Across the IP arena there are a variety of sources of useful information, all of which can help your management of intellectual property. Some of these are national organizations, some global. Some are business-focused firms while others are publications. We have selected several that can provide useful input to your organization.

Starting with intellectual property offices worldwide, we then focus on four key offices that have major roles: the USPTO, The Patent Office in the UK, WIPO and EPO; five industry bodies, IIPA, INTA, BSA, IFPI, and RIAA; five service providers, Aurigin, BTG, Delphion, The Patent and License Exchange, and QED; and, lastly, two publications, *Technology Review* and *Red Herring*.

INTELLECTUAL PROPERTY OFFICES WORLDWIDE

The first point of contact for any organization wishing to improve their IP management capability should be their local patent office. These are the fundamental resource which not only provide information on the specific approaches that may apply in a specific country but can also give local updates on any global issues. Below we have listed the URLs of all the key national property offices together with those of the two core international sources of reference: the European Patent Office and the World Patent Office.

Links

Australia: http://www.ipaustralia.gov.au
Austria: http://www.patent.bmwa.gv.at
Belgium: http://www.european-patent-office.org/patlib/country/belgium
Benelux
http://www.bmb-bbm.org
Brazil
http://www.inpi.gov.br
Denmark
http://www.dkpto.dk
Finland
http://www.prh.fi
France

http://www.inpi.fr
Germany
http://www.dpma.de
Greece
http://www.obi.gr
Ireland
http://www.european-patent-office.org/i.e.
Italy
http://www.european-patent-office.org/it
Japan
http://www.jpo-miti.go.jp
Korea
http://www.kipo.go.kr
Luxembourg
http://www.etat.lu/EC
Mexico
http://www.impi.gob.mx
The Netherlands
http://www.bie.minez.nl
Portugal
http://www.inpi.pt
Russia
http://www.rupto.ru
Spain
http://www.oepm.es
Sweden
http://www.prv.se
Switzerland
http://www.ige.ch
United Kingdom
http://www.patent.gov.uk
United States of America
http://www.uspto.gov
European Patent Office
http://www.european-patent-office.org
World Intellectual Property Organization
http://www.wipo.org

THE US PATENT AND TRADEMARK OFFICE

Of all the national patent offices, undoubtedly the most influential is the US patent office. Patents filed here are what organizations tend to take most notice of and, given the wider scope that exists here than in many of the other national offices, it is also where leading edge developments most frequently occur. The USPTO is a non-commercial federal entity and one of 14 bureaus in the US Department of Commerce (DOC). Based in Arlington, Virginia, it employs over 5,000 staff to support its major functions – the examination and issuance of patents and the examination and registration of trademarks.

The USPTO has evolved into a unique government agency. Since 1991 it has operated in much the same way as a private business, providing products and services to customers in exchange for fees that are used to fund its operations fully. The primary services provided include processing patents and trademarks and disseminating patent and trademark information. By disseminating both patent and trademark information, it seeks to promote an understanding of intellectual property protection and facilitate the developments and sharing of new technologies worldwide.

Link

http://www.uspto.gov/

THE PATENT OFFICE (UK)

Although the USPTO is now certainly the key national office in terms of filing IP, the UK patent office used to have this position and remains the one with the widest range of information and advice. The dedicated Website provides both introductory overviews and detailed procedures of how to file patent, trademark and design right applications in the UK, a historical perspective on each area, as well as downloadable information on all the latest developments in IP worldwide. A government-funded body like the USPTO, the UK patent office is operated as an independent entity.

Link

www.patent.gov.uk

WORLD INTELLECTUAL PROPERTY ORGANIZATION

The World Intellectual Property Organization (WIPO) is a single point of filing for global IP protection. It is an international organization dedicated to promoting the use and protection of intellectual property. With headquarters in Geneva, Switzerland, WIPO is one of the 16 specialized agencies of the United Nations system of organizations. It administers 21 international treaties dealing with different aspects of intellectual property protection. The number of member states belonging to WIPO now stands at 177, almost 90% of the world's countries – a reflection of the increasing importance and relevance attached to the work of the organization.

With a staff of some 760 drawn from around the world, WIPO carries out many tasks related to the protection of intellectual property rights, such as administering international treaties, assisting governments, organizations and the private sector, monitoring developments in the field and harmonizing and simplifying relevant rules and practices.

The PCT (Patent Co-operation Treaty) was established in 1970 to allow inventors to gain protection in a large number of countries by filing a single international patent application. There are currently 108 members of the PCT and the system is expanding rapidly, with the number of applications growing from 2,600 in 1979 to 74,000 in 1999.

Link

www.wipo.org

THE EUROPEAN PATENT ORGANIZATION

Established by the Convention on the Grant of European Patents signed in Munich 1973, the EPO is a uniform patent system in Europe. It is a single point of IP registration for the whole of the European Union. Created in 1977, the EPO is headquartered in Munich, with a branch in The Hague and sub-offices in Berlin and Vienna. The EPO is entirely self-financing from procedural and renewal fees.

Link

www.european-patent-office.org

INTERNATIONAL INTELLECTUAL PROPERTY ALLIANCE

The International Intellectual Property Alliance (IIPA) is a private sector coalition formed in 1984 to represent the US copyright-based industries in bilateral and multilateral efforts to improve international protection of copyrighted materials. IIPA is comprised of seven trade associations, each representing a significant segment of the US copyright community. These member associations represent over 1,500 US companies producing and distributing materials protected by copyright laws throughout the world – all types of computer software, including business applications software and entertainment software (such as videogame CDs and cartridges, personal computer CDs and multimedia products); motion pictures, television programs, DVDs and home videocassettes; music, records, CDs, and audiocassettes; textbooks, trade books, reference and professional publications; and journals (in both electronic and print media).

Its goal is a legal and enforceable regime for copyright that not only deters piracy, but also fosters technological and cultural progress in developing countries, and encourages local investment and employment. As technology rapidly changes, IIPA is working to ensure that high levels of copyright protection become a central component in the legal framework for the growth of global electronic commerce. To advance this goal, IIPA is working for the prompt ratification and effective implementation of the WIPO Copyright Treaty and the WIPO Performances and Phonograms Treaty in as many countries as possible.

Link
www.iipa.com

INTERNATIONAL TRADEMARK ASSOCIATION

The International Trademark Association (INTA) is a not-for-profit worldwide membership organization of trademark owners and advisors. INTA represents trademark owners to protect and advance the importance of trademarks as essential elements of international commerce. INTA shapes public policy, advances practitioners' knowledge and educates business, the media and the public on the significance of trademarks.

The group was originally organized as The United States Trademark Association on November 21, 1878 and played a key role in driving passage of the Trademark Act of 1881. INTA has changed significantly over the years, but it has remained true to its original purpose: to promote and support trademarks. INTA is the world's leading trademark association.

Link

www.inta.org

BUSINESS SOFTWARE ALLIANCE

The Business Software Alliance is an international organization representing leading software and e-commerce developers in 65 countries around the world. Established in 1988, BSA has offices in the United States, Europe, and Asia.

It aims to help governments and consumers understand how software strengthens the economy, worker productivity and global development; and how its further expansion hinges on the successful fight against software piracy and Internet theft. Its efforts include educating computer users about software copyrights; advocating public policy that fosters innovation and expands trade opportunities; and fighting software piracy.

Link

www.bsa.org

INTERNATIONAL FEDERATION OF THE PHONOGRAPHIC INDUSTRY

The IFPI is the organization representing the international recording industry. It comprises a membership of 1400 record producers and distributors in 76 countries. It also has national groups in 46 countries. IFPI's international Secretariat is based in London and is linked to regional offices in Brussels, Hong Kong, Miami and Moscow.

The IFPI Secretariat in London is responsible for coordinating international strategies in the key areas of the organization's work – anti-piracy enforcement, technology, lobbying of governments, and representation in international organizations, legal strategies, litigation and public relations. It is also the recording industry's most authoritative source of market research and information, providing a comprehensive range of global industry statistics.

IFPI's regional offices for Asia, the CIS countries, Europe and Latin America are responsible for implementing the Federation's strategies at regional level, co-ordinating the work of national groups, and setting lobbying priorities tailored to the political environment in their regions. IFPI is affiliated with the Recording Industry Association of America (RIAA), the organization responsible for the world's largest music market.

Link

www.ifpi.org

RECORDING INDUSTRY ASSOCIATION OF AMERICA

The Recording Industry Association of America is the trade group that represents the US recording industry. Its members are the record companies that comprise the majority of the US music industry. RIAA members create, manufacture and/or distribute approximately 90% of all legitimate sound recordings produced and sold in the United States. It works to protect intellectual property rights worldwide, and monitors and reviews state and federal laws, regulations and policies. The RIAA also certifies Gold, Platinum, and Diamond sales awards. It is active in the ongoing fight against music piracy in four areas.

» Pirate recordings – the unauthorized duplication of only the sound of legitimate recordings, as opposed to all the packaging, i.e. the original art, label, title, sequencing, combination of titles, etc.
» Counterfeit recordings – unauthorized recordings of the pre-recorded sound as well as the unauthorized duplication of original artwork, label, trademark, and packaging.
» Bootleg recordings – the unauthorized recordings of a live concert, or a musical broadcast on radio or television.
» Online piracy – the unauthorized uploading of a copyrighted sound recording and making it available to the public, or downloading a sound recording from an Internet site, even if the recording is not resold.

Link

www.riaa.org

AURIGIN

Aurigin Systems is a US-based consulting organization led by Kevin Rivette, author of *Rembrandts in the Attic* (see Chapter 8). Aurigin's Innovation Asset Solutions are based on a suite of dynamic analytic tools applied to a custom database of worldwide patents that allow customers to gain insight into their innovation asset opportunities.

Customers employ Aurigin's Innovation Asset Solutions to gain quick insight into their innovation asset management opportunities, and leverage these opportunities for a sustainable competitive advantage. Aurigin's Aureka platform tightly integrates a suite of iterative analytic tools with a knowledge base of worldwide patents. Users can easily create visualizations of their marketplace, their innovation assets, and their competitors' innovation assets.

Link

www.aurigin.com

DELPHION

In May of 2000, Internet Capital Group (ICG) and IBM announced the formation of a new, wholly independent company named Delphion. Delphion is a provider of intellectual asset management software and services that enable business and intellectual property professionals to research, manage, and analyze IP information to generate insight and extract the full value of their IP. The company's solutions are based on technologies originally developed by IBM that provide easy access to research, IP management and analytic tools that enable organizations to manage their IP assets strategically.

The Intellectual Property Network (IPN) began as an initiative within IBM. In 1997, in response to the growing need of individuals, organizations, and governments for more efficient methods of exploring intellectual property information, the IPN was made available to the public via the World Wide Web. With its expanded data coverage, it evolved into one of the most comprehensive sources for finding and viewing patent information. Today, the Delphion IPN is the world's most popular online destination for researching patents.

Delphion is headquartered in Chicago, Illinois, USA, with additional offices in San Jose, California, USA and The Netherlands.

Link

www.delphion.com

BTG

BTG, formerly the British Technology Group, is a technology commercialization organization operating in the UK, North America and Japan. It has over 50 years' experience in successfully commercializing important new technologies. The organization's approach of shared rewards maximizes the revenue generated for the sources of the technology, for those who bring it to market and for BTG. As a result it has formed strong relationships with many of the world's leading research centers as well as major technology companies.

By protecting and managing intellectual property rights (IPR) and enhancing technology through selective investment, BTG creates value from its portfolio of some 300 technologies. It aims to create a revenue stream through a variety of commercialization routes including licensing, incubating technology start-ups, and joint ventures.

Through its global reach BTG has access to many sources of inventions around the world. It works with universities and companies to determine the value of their technology portfolio and to identify ways in which they can make money from their IPR. Some companies prefer to initiate joint ventures and equity sharing arrangements, while others opt to assign their patented technologies to BTG for licensing. Once a product is launched BTG receives royalties on sales over the patent life, or gains from the equity appreciation in the investee companies. The organization monitors royalty obligations and has a forensic audit group that assesses and collects licensing revenues as appropriate. BTG shares revenues, including equity realizations, with the technology source.

The company claims to do much more than simply protect IPR, although this is a core competence. Its ability to add real value comes from the expertise in analyzing technological innovations to determine the steps in progressing towards product or service revenues. The company often brings together previously separate technologies to increase the potential of an existing portfolio. BTG looks for commercialization routes that create the greatest value, seeking out and sometimes creating companies which are best able to bring the product to market.

Link

www.btgplc.com

THE PATENT AND LICENSE EXCHANGE

The Patent and License Exchange is the first e-business marketplace for intellectual property rights. Founded in 1999, the pl-x.com marketplace was designed to transform powerful legal instruments into valuable financial assets. As the company has grown, it has attracted leaders in intellectual property, e-commerce, alternative risk transfer, and transaction assurance; and it has attracted the capital to transform these resources into a global e-commerce marketplace.

The government entities, businesses, law firms, consultancies and universities that comprise the pl-x.com subscriber base are required to go through a standard screening process prior to becoming a qualified member of this new marketplace. The pl-x.com marketplace aims to remove the risks and uncertainties associated with intellectual property transactions of the twentieth century. The marketplace provides information and risk management tools – tools standard to other disciplined financial markets – that help transform these valuable intangible assets – previously treated only as powerful legal instruments – into liquid financial instruments.

Link

www.pl-x.com

QED

Headquartered in the United Kingdom and with offices in both Japan and Sweden, QED is an intellectual property licensing company that provides licensing services to a range of international clients, helping them to generate income from their IP portfolios. QED's business is the commercial exploitation of intellectual assets and IP rights. It is the IP licensing arm of technology development and licensing company Scipher plc, and is responsible for securing the IP generated by Scipher's Central Research Laboratory Limited (CRL).

Historically linked with Thorn EMI, the company has been responsible for managing the IP rights of some groundbreaking technological firsts, including the electronic television, airborne radar, and the CAT Scanner. More recently it has been active in the fields of telecommunications, semiconductor applications, and the Internet.

Link

www.qed-ip.com

TECHNOLOGY REVIEW

Published by MIT, the *Technology Review* is a leading magazine providing insights into new technologies and emerging applications. With regular contributions from leading scientists as well as major business personalities, the *Technology Review* provides a clear, objective and authoritative point of view on issues that will impact future ideas. It regularly features items on patents and other forms of IP.

Link

http://www.technologyreview.com

RED HERRING

Launched in 1993, *Red Herring* magazine provides a forward-thinking, analytical look at technology companies and industries, and evaluates technology as a strategic asset. *Red Herring* magazine's content seeks to be timely, analytical, and skeptical. It aims to tell its readers ''what's first, what's new, and, most importantly, what matters.''

Link

www.redherring.com

Ten Steps for Managing Intellectual Property Successfully

How do you actually improve your ability to manage intellectual property? This final chapter outlines the key aspects that you need to focus on:

» put IP in context;
» assess your current IP position;
» determine what position you want;
» define your approach for building IP;
» find new sources of IP;
» build your IP portfolio;
» create value from your portfolio;
» build organizational capabilities;
» measure performance; and
» ensure that reviews happen.

1. PUT IP IN CONTEXT

Ensuring that, up front, you have a full and objective perspective of IP in context is the prerequisite for managing your own IP in an efficient and effective manner. The biggest problem with managing IP is that, due to the timescales involved, you cannot easily tell whether you are going in the right direction for some time. IP acquisition, development, exploitation and disposal is far from an instantaneous game and managing IP is a capability which itself has to be developed and refined. Fundamental to successful IP management is therefore a full understanding of the whole IP arena, free from sectoral bias and open to new developments.

While it is easy to perceive that what happens with IP in the aerospace and pharmaceutical industries may not, for example, be of relevance to the consumer goods sector, in reality the crossover impacts can be substantial. Whether associated with new composite materials and their product processes first used for helicopter rotor blades, or focused on where value-adding intellectual input to new drug development occurs to maximum tax advantage, the approaches to managing IP in both these areas can quite plausibly influence, say, Nike's position and strategy for protecting new technologies of the next generation of cross-trainers.

In addition, although not in itself evolving at light speed, recent changes in the IP world are having significant impact not only on the value of IP portfolios, but also on the approaches that organizations are taking to manage them. Issues such as the patenting of business methods, IP pooling, and software free from IP are having major, direct influence on many businesses and their revenue streams, and hence a good understanding of these developments and the potential impact on your business is vital. If you have never heard of patenting business methods, then maybe you ought to find out what the opportunities are and what is involved?

2. ASSESS YOUR CURRENT IP POSITION

As publicly acknowledged by the likes of both HP and Siemens, actually knowing what your organization knows is a major IP issue. Particularly in companies which have grown and diversified into multiproduct, multibusiness multinationals, but also in small and medium-sized technology-dependent firms, having a coherent view of what IP you do, or do not, own is an area in which few would claim a high degree of prowess. Moreover, to be aware of the *value* that either already resides in, or can potentially be delivered from, the exploitation of your existing IP, either within or outside your own business unit, company or even sector is an even rarer attribute.

As the second core step in developing the capability to managing your IP successfully, you must have a clear view of your current position. If you have IP within your organization, you must identify it and record it. To do so you may well have to conduct a detailed, in-depth audit. Only by drilling down to see which areas of your IP portfolio are effective in supporting your business activities, which aspects of your current activities are neither sufficiently protected nor being fully leveraged by IP, and what IP you own or have access to that has no impact or relevance to your organization, can you accurately define your starting point for effective IP management which can begin to deliver value.

3. DETERMINE WHAT POSITION YOU WANT

For many organizations, IP may well be a "nice to have" asset rather than a key enabler for business growth. Particularly in the service sector, where the key differentiators are price, quality, and efficiency of delivery of the customer experience, it has traditionally been sufficient to rely on internal know-how and experience to drive continued growth. Other than basic copyright and trademark protection, there may have been little leverage of IP.

However, even in the service sector things are changing, as the ability for others to mimic if not directly copy, increases. British Airways have had to protect and defend their flat beds from imitation, and in the Internet world Amazon's proprietary one-click process (as detailed in Chapter 4) has proven to be a core element in the future of book retailing. Even though in the past, secrecy of, say, product formulation has been sufficient protection for Coca-Cola and Kentucky Fried Chicken, in the future this certainly will not be enough.

Thus, even at the most basic level most organizations have to adopt a more effective defensive IP position. This may be right for you. For many other companies, however, a more aggressive IP stance is becoming a more regular requirement. Either to enable growth of existing business activities or to drive expansion into new areas, organizations as diverse as Sony, Merck, American Express, Oracle, BP, and Pizza Hut are all taking a far more aggressive approach to IP management, as they not only protect their current operations but more and more seek to populate, if not ring-fence, new opportunities for the future. Maybe this is where your organization should aim to be.

Alternatively, as displayed by Siemens, IBM, BT, and especially BTG, ARM, and Generics, you may even desire to move up the ladder to a position where you create, manage and exploit your IP as a core value generator to drive spin-outs, licensing revenues or even pure investment vehicles.

Whichever of these three stances is right for you and your business within the context of your sector, you have to make a clear choice as to which, or how many, of these you want to be in for the future.

4. DEFINE YOUR APPROACH FOR BUILDING IP

Having determined both an accurate view on your current IP position, and also what position you wish to have, step 4 in successfully managing your IP is focused on defining the most appropriate strategy to make this transition. For some companies with little or no existing IP portfolio, this may well be largely a matter of defining an approach for creating an initial critical mass of patents, trademarks and design rights around which a stronger long-term position can be created. For organizations with an existing portfolio, this could focus more on reviewing current assets, and pruning or adding to the IP to create a more coherent position for the future.

Whatever your stance, with clarification of your existing position from step 2 and your definition of what future IP position you wish to have from step 3, you can identify the key gaps that need to be filled. Whether in terms of geographic reach, type of protection or level of coverage, you can determine what needs to be done, and, through breaking this down into realistic chunks, define key milestones over a two- to five-year period. Underpinning these key steps in the evolution of your IP position, three component activities have to be defined – what IP to sell, what IP to create, and what IP to acquire.

Together these three inter-related activities require a coherent and co-ordinated strategy that ensures efficient evolution of the IP position of the organization. However, in the fast-changing world of IP where a move by a competitor can significantly undermine your position and your approach, the strategy has to be regularly reviewed in the light of the developing IP landscape around your business.

5. FIND NEW SOURCES OF IP

A core element in the building and managing of an IP portfolio is the ability to access IP from outside the organization. For many companies, irrespective of their size, reach or industrial sector, external sources of IP can be both a quick and rich supply of the key levels of protection and value generation that may be required. Typical sources of external IP fall into three core categories:

» universities and other research organizations;
» IP-rich companies outside your sector; and
» competitors and collaborators within your sector.

Details of what IP exists and may therefore be available across all three of these categories can best be acquired through undertaking an external audit, primarily through patent searches around key target technologies and areas of application. Either by engaging patent attorneys or commissioning a search directly from the relevant patent office, a list of patents either applied for or granted can provide you with a detailed insight into the areas in which other organizations have been developing new technologies. Also, by comparing these to their current areas of activity, a search can help identify in what areas their future growth might be. In addition, citation trees, which link one patent to another through citation as prior art can be useful identifiers of others' activities. Moreover by not only recognizing the corporations which own particular IP, but by also identifying the actual originators of key inventions in person, it is possible to track their career movement and create opportunities for gaining access to their knowledge.

Only by ensuring that you have a good understanding of others' IP portfolios can both the positive and negative impacts on your strategy for evolving your IP position be determined. An effective IP manager has a very good idea of not only what IP exists external to his organization, but also what may be available either through purchase, license or swap. Armed with this knowledge the tactical stance on how best to fulfill the organization's IP strategy can be both formulated and executed.

6. BUILD YOUR IP PORTFOLIO

Having determined the approach for improving your IP position, and identified potential external sources, the sixth step is to build your core IP portfolio. This means protect the IP you have with the right tools, and either license or buy-in the missing pieces.

Key to building your IP is to use the right tools. If, for example, you are a streaming company providing multimedia services to organizations that want to broadcast conferences or meetings via the Internet, either live or on demand, then you potentially need to protect the following core IP:

» enabling software, either through patent and/or copyright;
» corporate name, logo, and strap-line through trade marks and service marks;
» Website, marketing collateral, and any manuals through copyright; and
» any packaging with design registration.

Furthermore, if you wish to offer a fully end-to-end service by also operating in the mobile arena, you may also need to acquire licenses for:

» mobile connectivity from Qualcomm;
» wireless applications from Bluetooth; and
» music distribution from MusicNet or PressPlay.

In addition, there may be opportunities to buy core IP that will underpin your competitive position from suppliers or failed competitors.

Whatever the scenario, there is a minimal IP portfolio which an organization requires to compete in certain arenas and this has to be built, in as effective and coherent a manner as possible.

7. CREATE VALUE FROM YOUR PORTFOLIO

With an IP portfolio in place, and a strategy defined for growing it over time, step 7 is to create value from it.

From a defensive perspective, certain IP you hold has to be maintained and monitored to underpin internal business growth, value creation and your competitive position. Largely a matter of applying for new protection to cover new areas of operation, filing updates and watching for infringements, this is an activity which is best outsourced to a specialist patent agent or attorney who can provide you with the necessary information when required, but will not demand too great an internal resource.

From a growth perspective, there are four means by which you can generate value:

Sell

For non-core IP you can use citation trees and patent searches to find out which companies are operating close to or within the same arena as your organization, and who may therefore wish to acquire the ownership of any relevant IP.

License

For core IP, critical to your business, there may be some IP that can best be used to create a wider customer base or to define a new technology standard. Whether this necessitates franchising of your business model and trade marks, or licensing of your core technology patents, this is the most effective manner of generating external revenue that simultaneously supports your long-term business growth.

Spin-out

The third option is to create spin-outs to exploit non-core but well-positioned IP. As companies seek to focus on their core activities, and drive growth through concentrating the majority of resource on key technologies and markets, rather than sell, more and more firms are taking the spin-out option. Whether through an internal incubator, a separate business unit or a flotation, companies such as BT, Xerox, Generics, and others are all pursuing this approach.

Internal exploitation

Lastly, through identifying other applications within your organization or allied business units for IP within your portfolio, you can exploit your IP internally. Where possible, it is far more efficient to reuse existing IP than to create anew, and thus any cross-business sharing is also an ideal means of generating value.

8. BUILD ORGANIZATIONAL CAPABILITIES

In order to build your ability to maximize the value from your intellectual capital and, as its tangible asset, the associated IP portfolio, there are certain IP capabilities that have to be developed.

At a basic skills level, it is highly likely that it will be necessary to hire new staff with a proven track record to take leadership roles. Recruiting expertise from large high technology companies or media giants is the route many take. Alternatively, for the short term, sub-contracting IP management to one of the few specialist firms is always an option, although this has to be an interim and not the long-term solution.

For existing resource, the key advancements in learning and understanding of IP and the issues surrounding it is acquired through awareness training that is available from government or international patent offices. Other providers are currently few and far between.

That said, skills are not the be-all and end-all in this arena, for new skills are largely redundant without structure and, for some firms, successfully managing IP can require a fundamental change. There has to be an IP-centric culture and focus within and across the organization. This can be achieved through creating a dedicated, high profile team or, alternatively, by driving IP development down into everyone's motivation and reward systems. Whichever approach is taken, a transparent and effective process to underpin the structure, and drive focus, progression, and exploitation, of IP is vital.

9. MEASURE PERFORMANCE

As with any major organizational enhancement, IP management performance has to be assessed and key to this are appropriate measures. Targets drive behavior and behavior drives results. Typical key performance indicators, or KPIs, adopted in leading organizations include:

» % revenue generated from IP licensing; and
» # patents granted.

Both of these are output-focused. By contrast:

» time to royalty; and
» % cross-business utilization of IP

are internal drivers that encourage focus and reuse of IP, that both improve sharing and reduce IP management costs.

Together these all provide a set of metrics by which R&D activities can be evaluated in more commercial terms, and through which valid comparative benchmarking with competitors can be undertaken.

10. ENSURE THAT REVIEWS HAPPEN

As mentioned in step 1, IP performance is not instantaneous. It takes time to embed an IP-centric culture and, other than from selling non-core IP, revenue streams can take a while to hit the P&L. Step 10 in successfully managing IP is to ensure that you regularly review both your performance and your strategy.

The metrics identified in step 9 provide the mechanism by which quarterly or, more realistically, annual performance can be judged and measured against both plan and the competition. Equipped with the associated analysis:

» under-performing IP assets can be re-evaluated and subsequent decisions can be taken to sell or discard specific patents, design rights, etc.;
» fundamental IP which is creating a key building block for the future can be highlighted and provision made for its maintenance and strengthening; and
» new applications of core IP can also be explored, and possible licensing opportunities identified.

Together with an annual review of IP strategy and approach, frequent updating on changes in the overall IP management as identified in step 1 all helps to drive a virtuous circle where new approaches can be tested, and lessons learned and acted upon to help achieve a continuous improvement in performance.

Frequently Asked Questions (FAQs)

Q1: Why is managing intellectual property important?
A: Chapter 1: Introduction.

Q2: How do I know what IP I have?
A: Chapter 2: Managing IP; Chapter 10: steps 2 & 3.

Q3: How do I gain value from my IP?
A: Chapter 2: Managing IP; Chapter 7: In Practice;
Chapter 10: Ten Steps.

Q4: How does the Internet impact on IP?
A: Chapter 4: The E-Dimension.

Q5: How do we protect and exploit IP abroad?
A: Chapter 5: The Global Dimension.

Q6: How can we improve our IP performance?
A: Chapter 6: State of the Art; Chapter 7: In Practice; Chapter 10: Ten
Steps.

Q7: How do I best organize for IP management?

A: Chapter 2: Managing IP; Chapter 10: step 9.

Q8: Where can I go for help?

A: Chapter 9: Resources.

Q9: Who are the experts in taking ideas to market?

A: Chapter 7: In Practice; Chapter 8: Key Concepts and Thinkers.

Q10: What are the critical success factors for managing IP?

A: Chapter 10: Ten Steps.

Acknowledgments

The authors would like to thank Wendy and Anna for their patience, encouragement, editing and feedback.

Index